Antonio López

*This book would not have seen the light of day without the kind
assistance offered by the artist himself and by his daughter,
María López Moreno, whom we must also thank for providing
the illustrations required.*

Antonio López

Ediciones Polígrafa

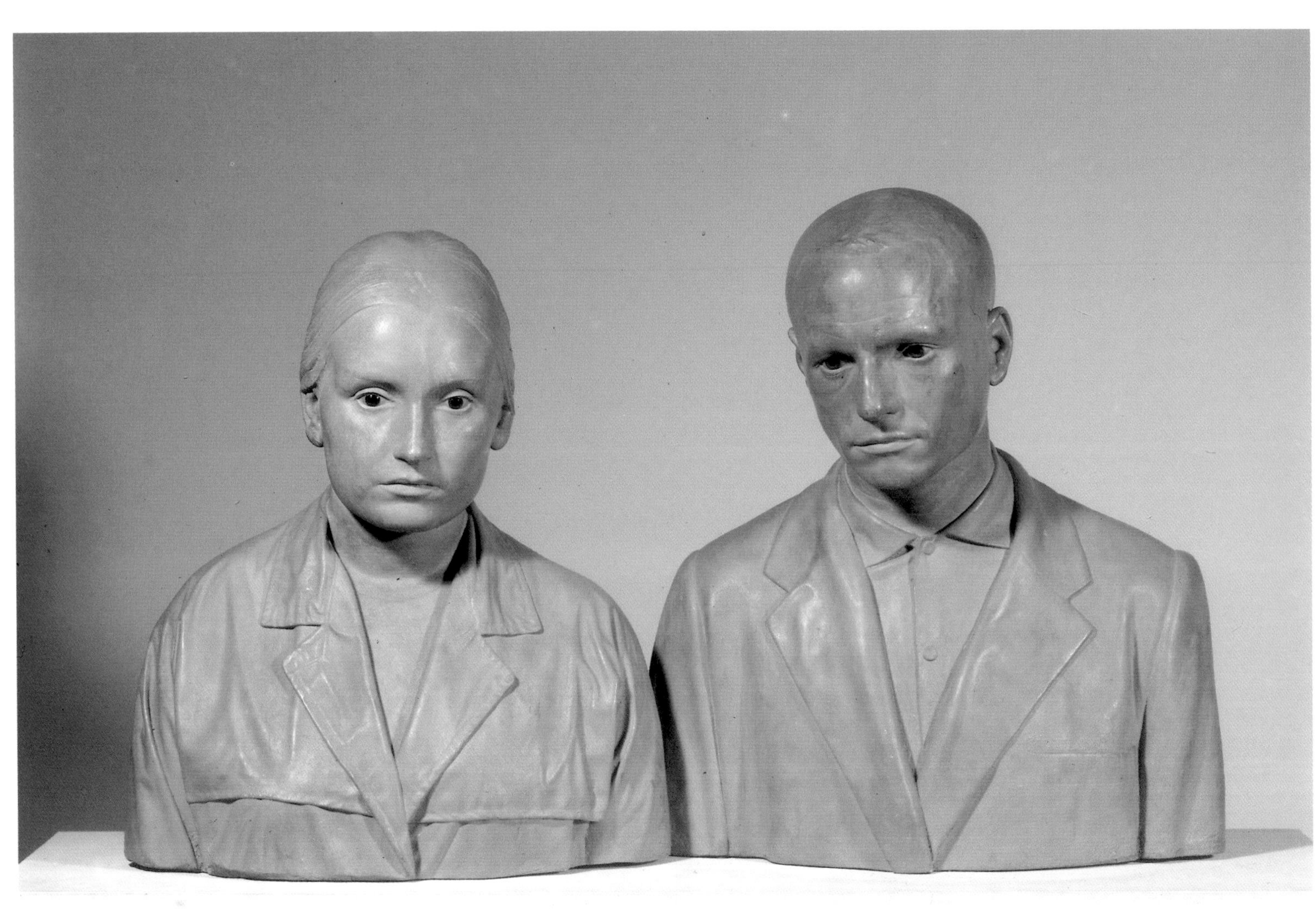

Antonio and Mari, 1967–1968
Polychromed wood.
Man: 55 × 47 × 28 cm; Woman: 51.5 × 45.5 × 28 cm.
Städtische Kunstsammlungen, Darmstadt

Antonio López García.
The meaning of reality

The figure of Antonio López could well be associated with those of a select number of painters — Bacon and Balthus are the finest examples — who, in a century dominated by various avant-garde trends and their legacy, have constructed their oeuvre on the margins of this tradition. This marginal stance does not of course preclude contaminations and various connections with this language, although it has conditioned his trajectory in two ways. On the one hand, his career has been a solitary one, unprecedented in the contemporary art scene, and on the other, it does not fit neatly into the historiographical categories derived from the avant-garde tradition; as a result, some authors have called into question the modernism of his oeuvre.

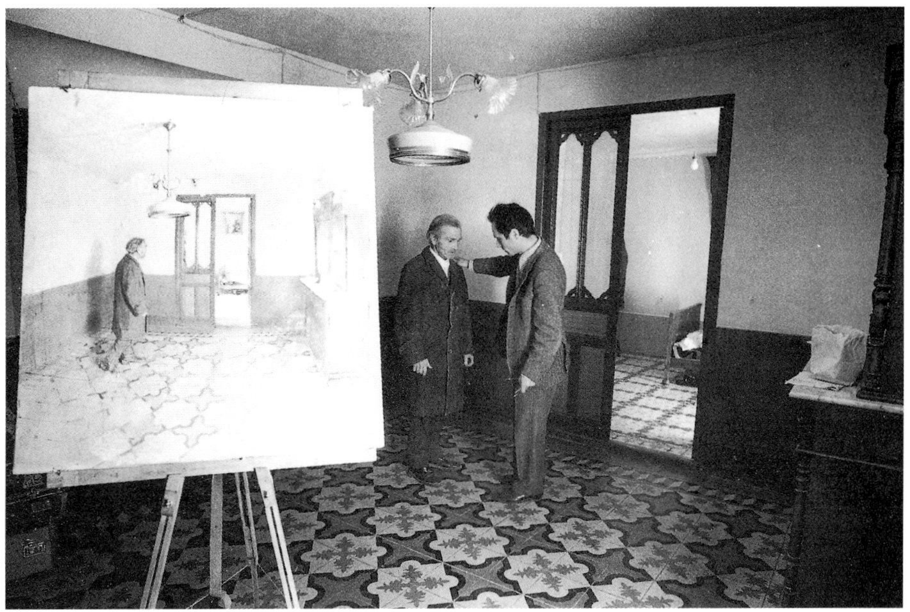

Antonio López working on the drawing of his uncle, Antonio López Torres at his house in Tomelloso in 1973. Photo: Moses.

Reality and Mystery

Antonio López is a Realist painter and, as such, aspires to create a faithful pictorial testimony of the world around him — the city in which he lives, the intimate spaces and insignificant objects of his personal environment. However, during the early period of his career (from 1957 to 1964 approximately) his works would be characterised by an inclination to fantasy we could well describe as Surrealist. Although he would abandon this line of research around the mid sixties, its very existence reveals a desire to disclose deeper meanings than those involved in representation. Indeed, art critics always stress this undercurrent of mystery, this aspiration to the absolute revealed by his painting; the question is to determine its actual nature.

Antonio López has always expressed certain nostalgia for the times when artists merged into a system of generally accepted collective values of which they were simply the conveyors. At previous moments in the history of art this group of signs and codes ensured the integration of artistic production in its social context — in short, the meaning of reality was the same for artists and audiences alike. This nostalgia explains the Castilian painter's love of ancient Greek sculpture and Egyptian carvings. He has always admired the Louvre's *The Seated Scribe* for instance, the technical shortcomings of which he overlooked as a consequence of the inventive way in which it conveys a fragment of everyday life in Pharaonic Egypt; its anonymous author disappearing in the light of the skilful expression of shared collective values.

Fragmented Reality

In our times such a shared global vision is no longer possible. "Reality has a highly resonant physical appearance that twentieth-century man perceives

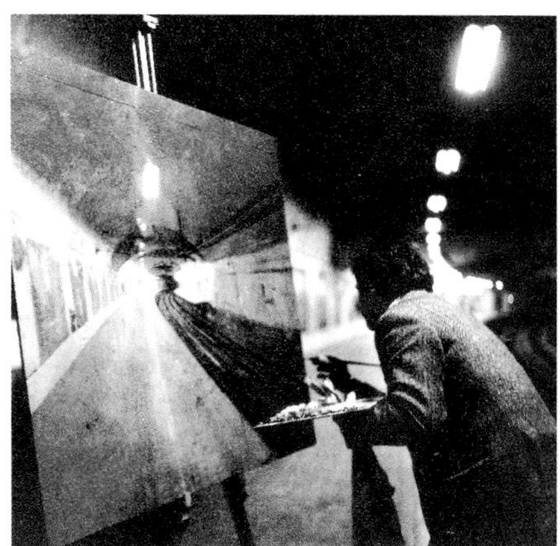

As a result of his growing interest in Madrid as a pictorial motif, in 1972 Antonio López placed his easel in one of the Metro stations to capture the atmosphere of the city's underbelly. Photo: Gilbert Lloyd.

Since the seventies the artist has felt an increasing need to work with his motif permanently in front of him. Photo: Imanol Sistiaga.

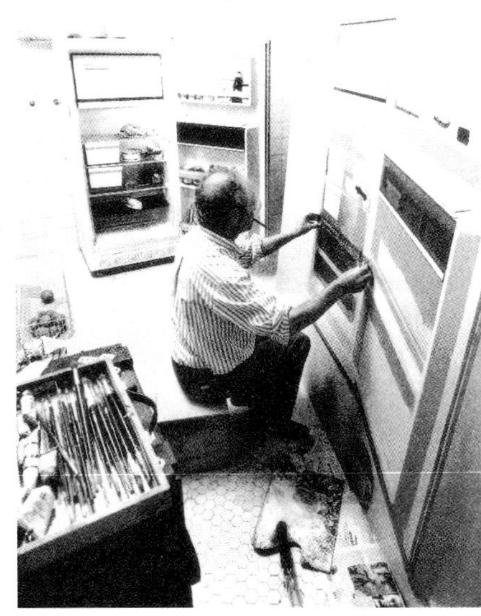

from different angles to those distinctive of other ages," the artist told Michael Brenson in 1989, to explain the fragmentation of the unitary and universal notion of reality characterising the modern world. In this frame of mind, the only certainty of the painter who intends to provide a faithful record of reality is the phenomenal condition of reality, the certainty of what he is seeing and of the possibility of sharing this perceptive act with his fellow men. It is interesting to note here that the most obvious measure of the evolution of Antonio López' oeuvre is his increasing dependency on the motif. In 1957 he was still able to draw in charcoal a large frieze such as *Four Women*, in which the characters are entirely the fruit of his imagination, bearing no resemblance whatsoever to any real model. Years later the painter would require a continuous vision of his motif, which strictly conditioned his subject matter. This marks the onset of his legendary slowness, leading to pictures painstakingly painted for years on end, cityscapes meticulously recreated at specific hours, days and seasons, and always under very precise lighting conditions.

Presences and Meanings

As in the still lifes by Zurbarán or Sánchez Cotán, this precise way of recreating the perceptible details of everyday objects affords them such an expressive intensity that they become quite disturbing. As Calvo Serraller has observed, this "excess significance of the insignificant" tends to make one think that the emphasis cannot be unwarranted, but must somehow conceal something elusive, mysterious and non-apprehensible. This is the link between Antonio López and the anti-classicist tradition of seventeenth-century Naturalism in Spanish painting. The works by Velázquez for instance, greatly admired by López, provoke the same tension between the clarity of the figures and the enigma of meanings that easily escape our gaze. In López, the awareness of confronting a fragmentary reality goes hand in hand with the uncertainty surrounding the very limits of pictorial language: the old masters did not only face up to an *established* reality, but did so following pictorial conventions in which they and their public had blind faith.

The Veneer of Time

The avant-garde destroyed the idea of a unique language, of one single legitimate form of representation. This explains why the artist's procedure before the canvas is not systematic, why he makes no preparatory studies — each stage of the work is the outline of the next, in a permanent superimposition of time. López conceives the execution of the picture as a bitter struggle with his motif, always on board or a pre-stretched canvas, for he needs "the surface to be rigid and consistent, in order for it to withstand all that will follow (…). The process is a long unpremeditated struggle with the language of painting, continually adding and taking away matter until the surface, the veneer, acquires an expressiveness which, when added to the other components forming the picture, matches what I see." The painting is therefore a surface on which time is deposited as a continuous present (the extended present of the execution), in which the motif never out of sight — an impossible time. This impossibility preserves the mystery of the absolute that surfaces and yet is never captured in these works, where everything seems to linger in such close proximity.

Antonio López García

Antonio López was born in Tomelloso, a large rural town of La Mancha, in the heart of Spain, a few months before the outbreak of the Spanish Civil War in 1936. As the eldest of four children in well-to-do family of farmers, young Antonio was supposed to follow in the family footsteps. However, the ease with which he soon took to drawing was soon detected by his uncle Antonio López Torres, a local landscape painter who gave him his first art lessons, thanks to whom his parents approved Antonio's decision to dedicate himself to painting. Barely thirteen, Antonio moves to Madrid to prepare his examination to enter the Fine Arts School.

Postwar Madrid

From 1950 to 1955 Antonio López proves himself a brilliant student, and is awarded a number of prizes. His friends and acquaintances are fellow students at the school: the painters María Moreno (whom he would marry in 1961), Lucio Muñoz and Enrique Gran (who subsequently turned to Abstraction), and the sculptors Julio and Francisco López Hernández. The artistic affinity between the latter, Amalia Avia, Isabel Quintanilla and Antonio López himself was such that in the sixties they would be described as Realists, in spite of their declarations to the contrary. Postwar Madrid was isolated from the international art scene, and the information about modern and even classic art available to Antonio López at the time was limited to the reduced number of illustrated books available at the art school's library, and to the volumes printed in Argentina that passed from hand to hand. This was probably his introduction to the work of Picasso and of other great figures of the avant-garde. In 1955 Antonio López is awarded a grant that enables him to travel to Italy with Francisco López, where he is somewhat disappointed by Italian Renaissance painting (a style he had until then admired), and begins to reappraise the Spanish painting he had been fortunate to study in depth at the Prado, particularly Velázquez who, alongside Vermeer, would be a perpetual referent in his oeuvre.

Magic Realism

The categorical definition of volume in his early works (*Josefina Reading*, 1953) reveals the influence of the Italian quattrocento. His concern regarding plastic solidity and precise composition stimulates his interest in Cézanne and Cubism (*Women Looking at Aeroplanes*, 1954), and in subject matter related to his family environment in Tomelloso. In 1957 his work will adopt a Surrealist note, as his canvases begin to be peopled with de-contextualised

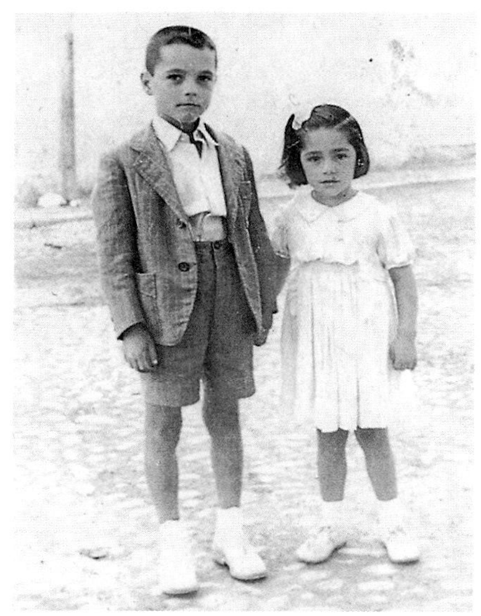

A picture of Antonio López (aged seven) and his sister Josefina in Tomelloso, his Castilian birthplace, a town with which he has always kept close ties even after settling in Madrid in 1961.

Antonio López Torres painting with Antonio López García, María Moreno, Isabel Quintanilla and her son, Francisco López Quintanilla, in 1974. Photo: Moses.

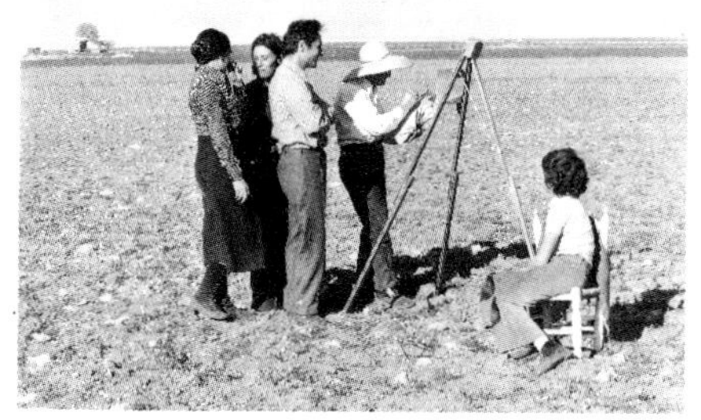

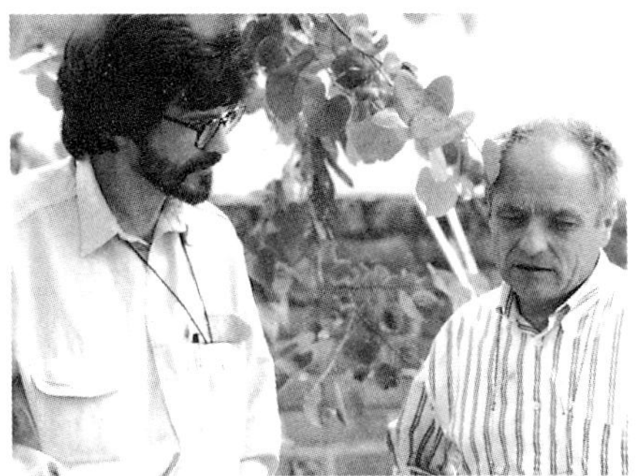

Antonio López with Victor Erice, director of the film El sol del membrillo *in which the filmmaker describes the painter's arduous fight against reality and time.*

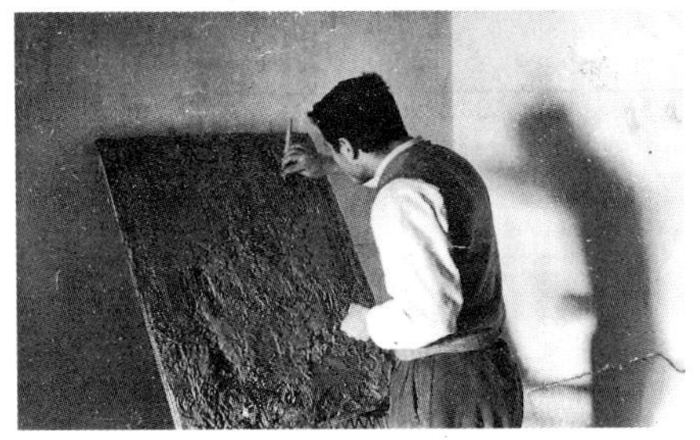

The artist in 1955 modelling his first relief. Since then his sculptural work has tended to focus on the human figure.

A meaningful picture of the painter resting in his studio, taken in 1988.

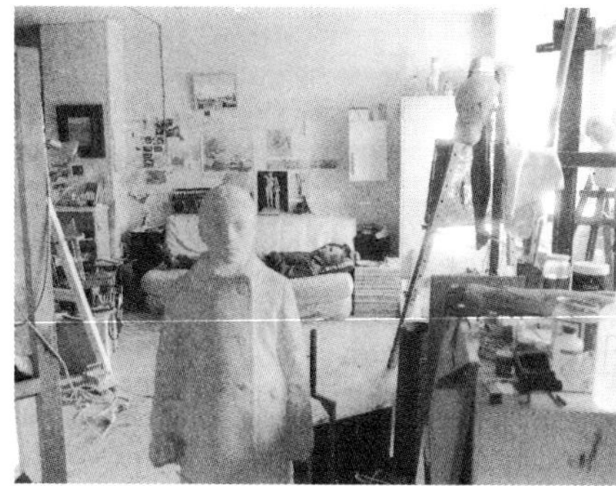

figures and objects floating in space; his pictorial language, however, still embodies the tactile volumetric classicism of his early works. The inclination to vagary will continue to be present, at least until 1964 (it is still discernible in *Atocha*, completed that year), although from 1960 onwards it will lose intensity. The number of works in which he resorts to fantasy will gradually decrease, and narrative content will begin to lose ground in favour of greater accuracy of representation. In fact the painter seems to depend increasingly on his motif, preferring to have it constantly in view to be able to recreate its finest details. This double aspect of his work during this period was paralleled by the critical acclaim he obtained in the sixties and seventies categorised as Magic Realism, a term the artist has always considered superfluous. The fact is that his pictures and drawings did seem to be progressively approaching the "sense of density of what we define as the visual world", to quote Brenson, translated into a minute and almost obsessive recreation of motif.

An Intense Gaze

The streets in Tomelloso would be followed by panoramic views of Madrid (the first of which dates back to 1960) that would soon after configure one of the most well-known and remarkable features of his oeuvre. His work begins to merit official recognition, first on a national scale (in 1961 he holds his first solo exhibition at a commercial gallery in Madrid) and shortly afterwards in an international context (in 1965 and 1968 his works are on display at New York's Staempfli Gallery). As always, Antonio López is attracted to commonplace subject matter — domestic interiors and exteriors, images of his wife and two daughters, anonymous everyday objects, desolate vistas and garden scenes — and yet the presence of his motifs is evermore precise, intense and even enigmatic. The execution of his pictures is progressively drawn out (in some cases a painting can be worked on for over twenty years and then abandoned without him considering it finished), consequently in spite of his continuous and complete dedication his production is not too extensive.

Solitary Triumph

For most of his career Antonio López has worked virtually alone, immersed in an art scene that was influenced by Abstraction and *Art Informel*, and later on by Conceptual Art. During the sixties and much of the seventies his reputation grew silently and he held a small number of few exhibitions that proved quite successful. It is difficult to ascertain convincing ties between his oeuvre and the new figurative trends in European art, as it is to establish any connection with American Hyper-Realism. Up until the eighties Antonio López held very few solo exhibitions, although mention should be made of those organised in Paris and Turin in 1972, and of a second Parisian show in 1997. In 1985 his work is displayed in an anthological exhibition at the Museo de Albacete, and in a retrospective show held in Brussels on occasion of Europalia '85. The following year two shows organised in New York and London pave the way for the great anthology held in 1993 at Madrid's Museo Nacional Centro de Arte Reina Sofía, which definitively establishes his reputation on a worldwide scale.

Plates

The Human Presence

Save for a few exceptions, the portraits and pictures by Antonio López usually represent members of his family or of his closest circle of friends. Such works abound in the first half of his career, from which time on he prefers to explore the human figure in sculpture. The poses of the models depicted in his earliest compositions are not too expressive, as if the painter preferred to resort to a collective iconographic memory, without of course forsaking the individual identities of his sitters to the point of granting them anonymity. The tension between generic and concrete traits in his sitters is a general stylistic feature of his works in this genre. Antonio López has always acknowledged his interest in the tactile value of figures, in their volume and free-standing nature — not in vain would he later pursue the same motifs in sculptures in the round. So, the characters he portrays are always solid presences, although they do not attain that monumental quality we discover in other painters who approach the same subject matter following the same principles.

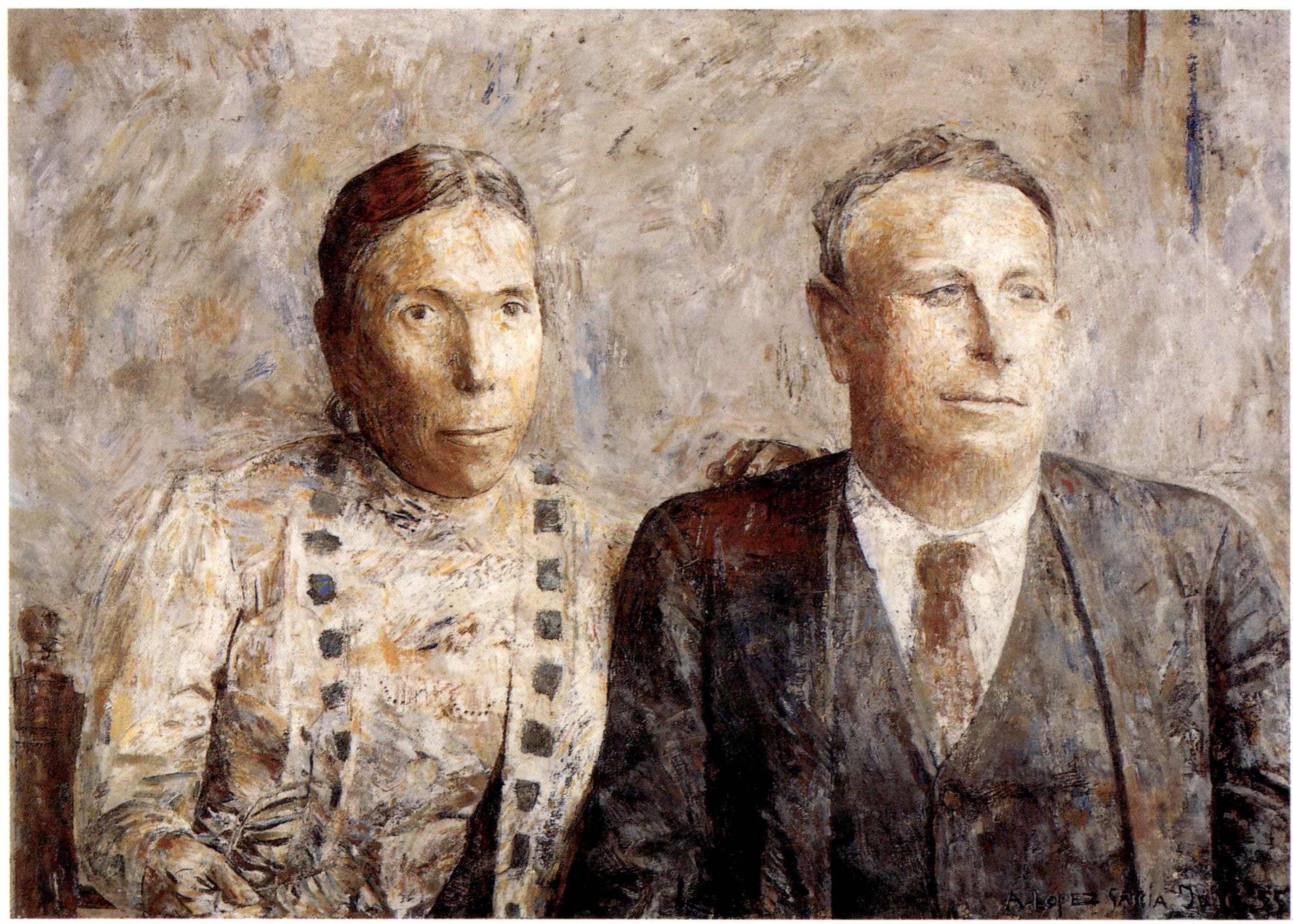

1

1-2. Sinforoso and Josefa, *1955.*
Antonio and Carmen, *1956. Two
double portraits of the artist's
grandparents, recalling the typical
frozen poses of the first photographs
that required long exposures. In these
works Antonio López attempts to
establish a connection with a specific
iconography stored in collective
memory. The instruments chosen to
model volume in such a compact way
are colour and impasto, that award
the figures a certain classical
quality.*

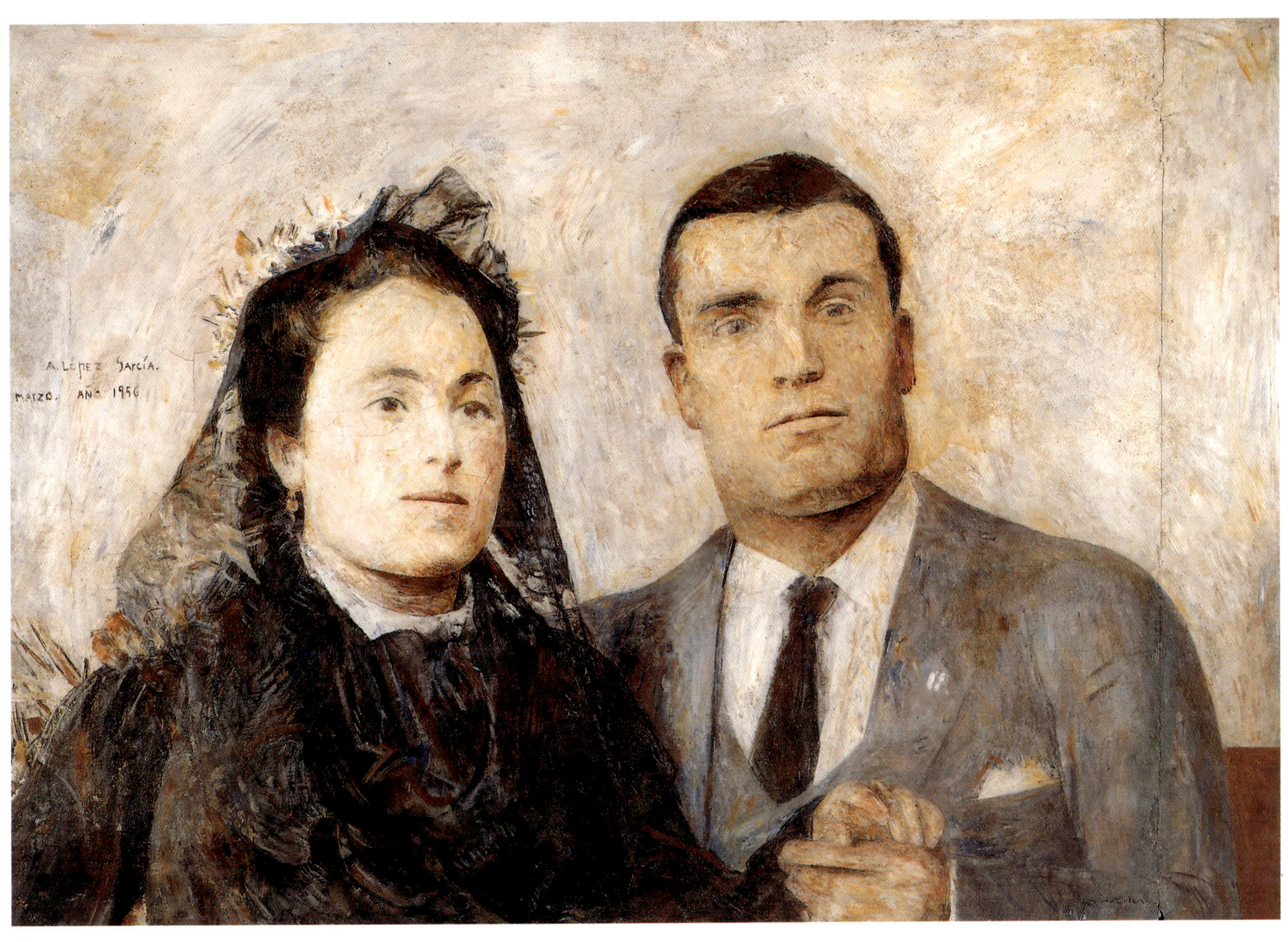

2

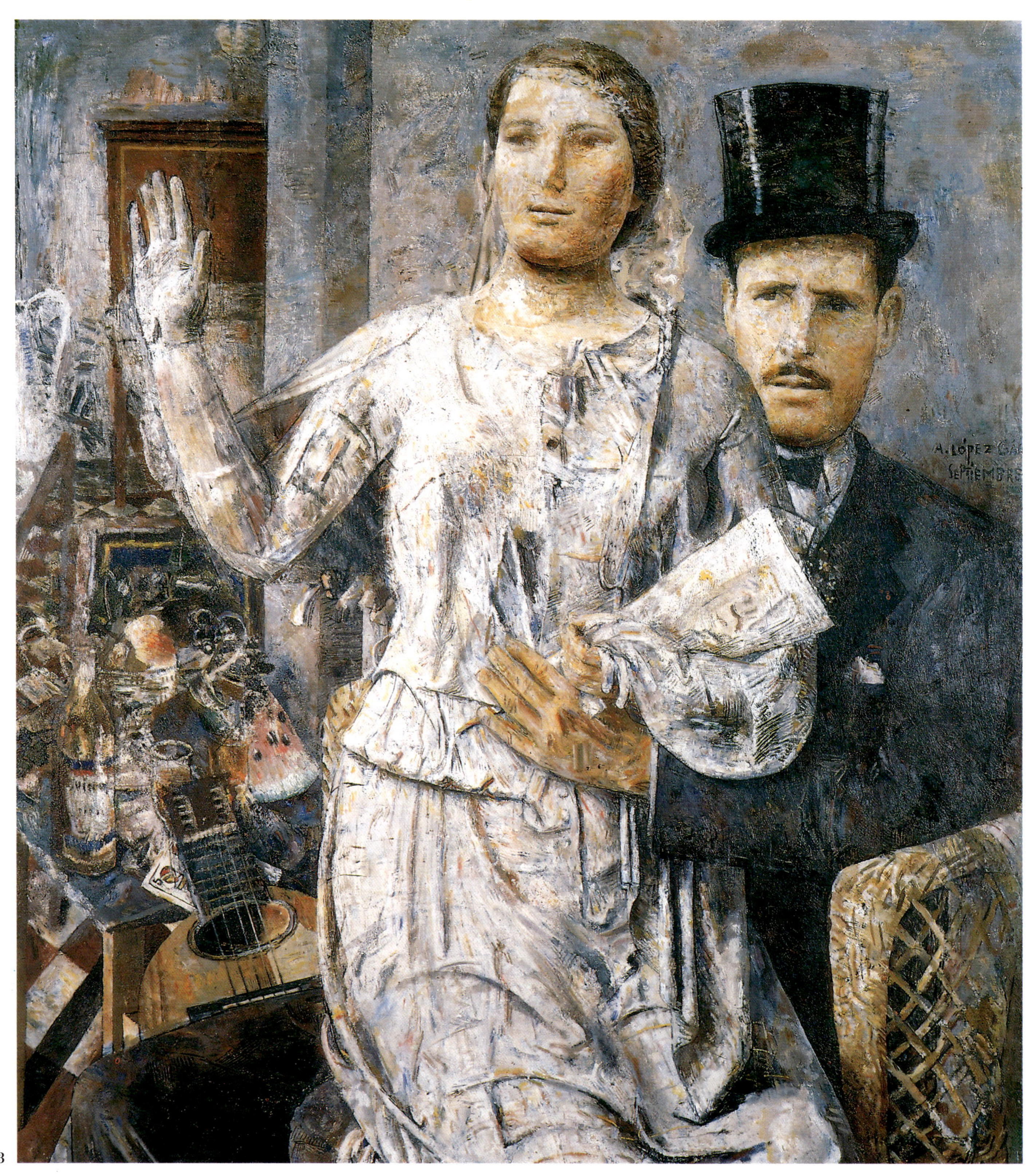

3

3. The Bride and Groom, *1955. While the
two figures preserve a certain hieratic
rigidity, as exemplified by their frozen
gestures, the still life on the left is
characterised by a Cézannesque, even Cubist
language, presenting intersecting planes of
colour revolving around a focal point. The
still life provides a local touch and a cheerful
contrast to the solemnity of the figures.*

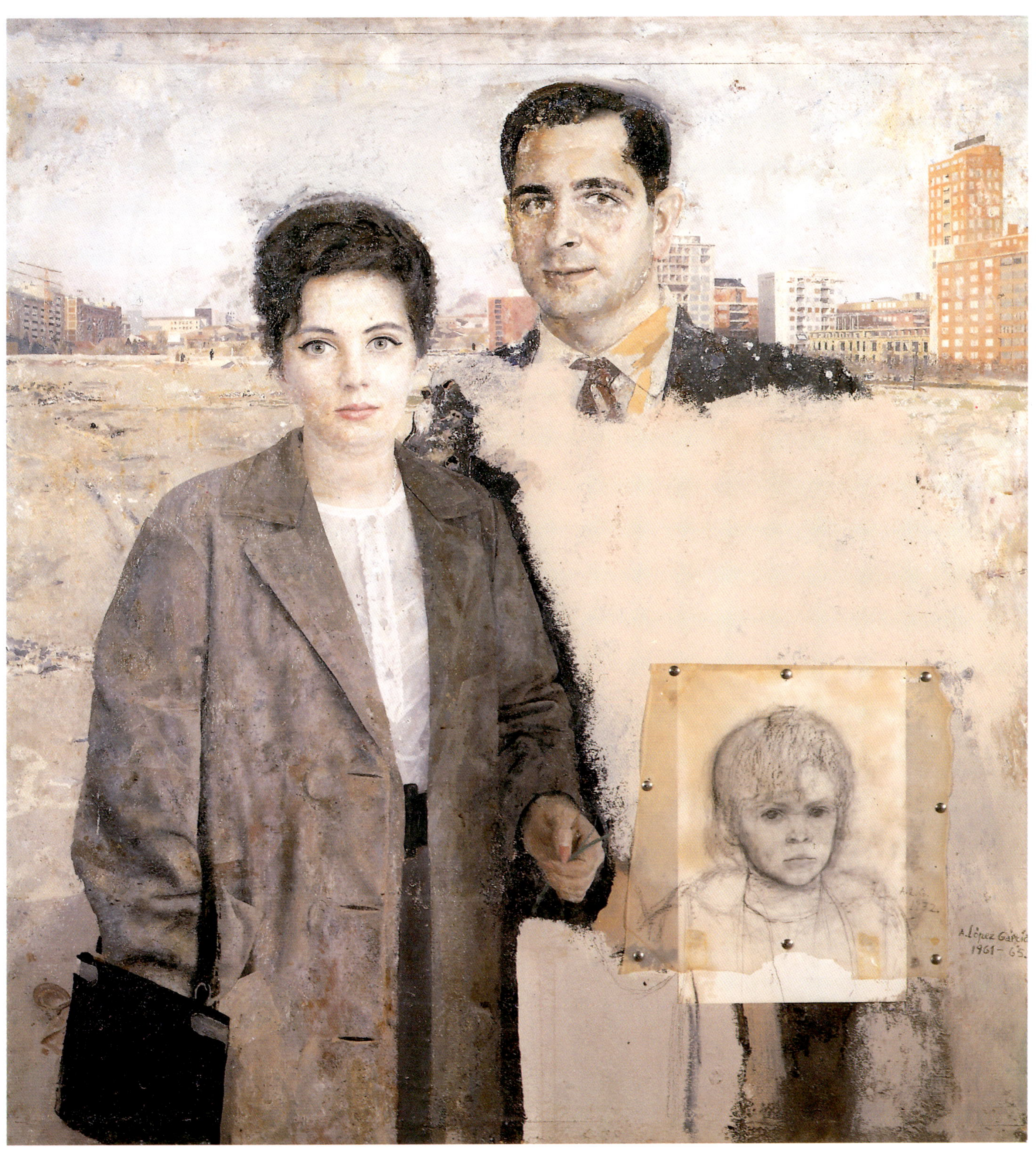

4. Emilio and Angelines, *1961–1965. Comparing this work
with the artist's early portraits of couples we find it easy
to trace the new direction his oeuvre took in the sixties.
The four years López spent on the picture, leaving
Emilio's figure uncompleted, account for the drawing of
the child. The urban landscape in the background draws a
parallel with the vistas of Madrid the painter was working
on at this time, and also provides a context for the couple,
possibly newly-weds who have just settled in one of the
city's emerging districts.*

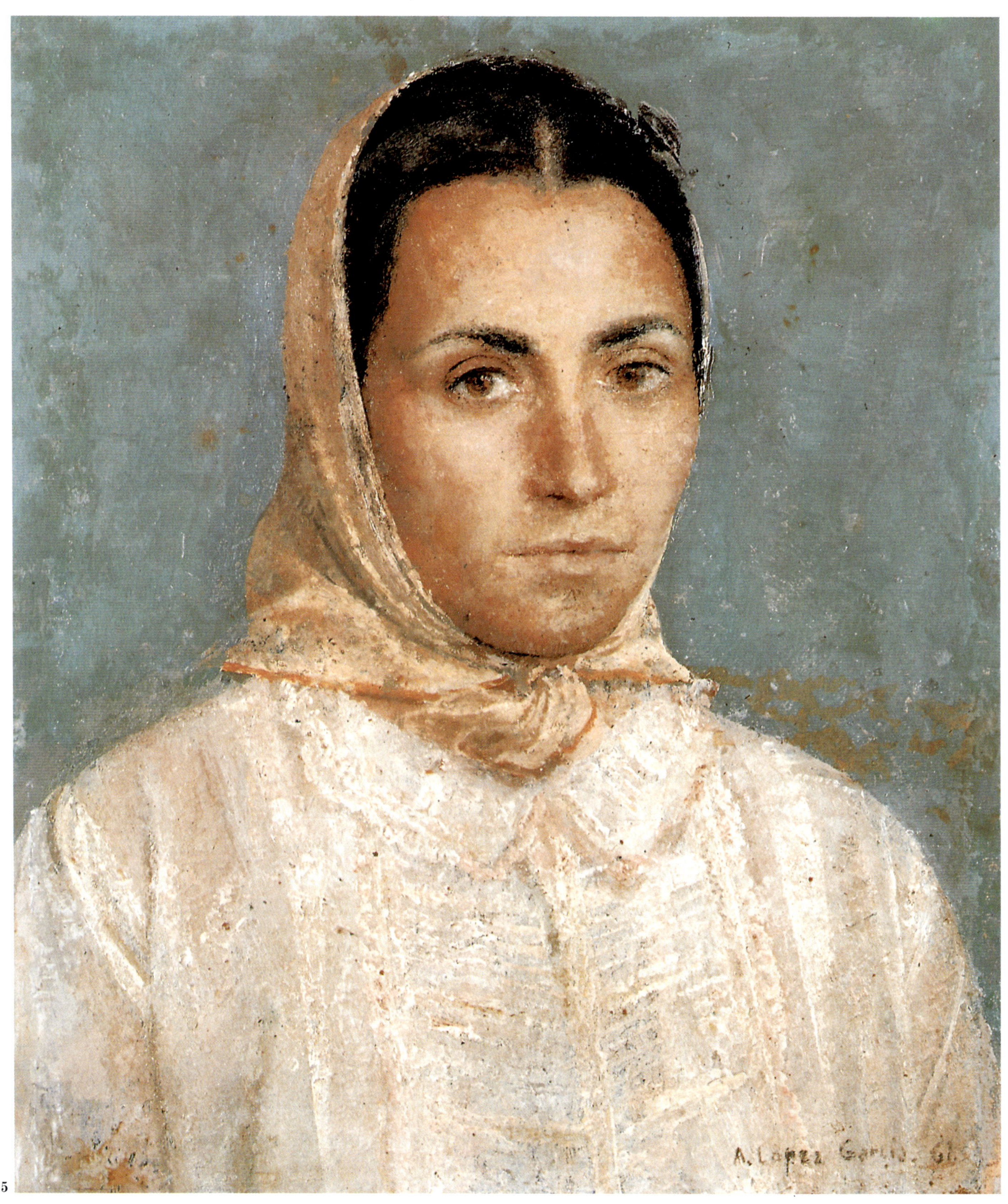

5

5. Mari, *1961. This portrait of María Moreno was painted the same year in which she married Antonio López. It is one of the few paintings that bear relation to a preparatory sketch, also produced in 1961. The corporeal quality of the figure derives from the comparison between the oval shape of her face and that of her headscarf, both of which are quite distinct and hark back to the painters of the Italian quattrocento, in particular Piero della Francesca. The painstaking application of matter to recreate form is a characteristic feature of the artist's Realist works.*

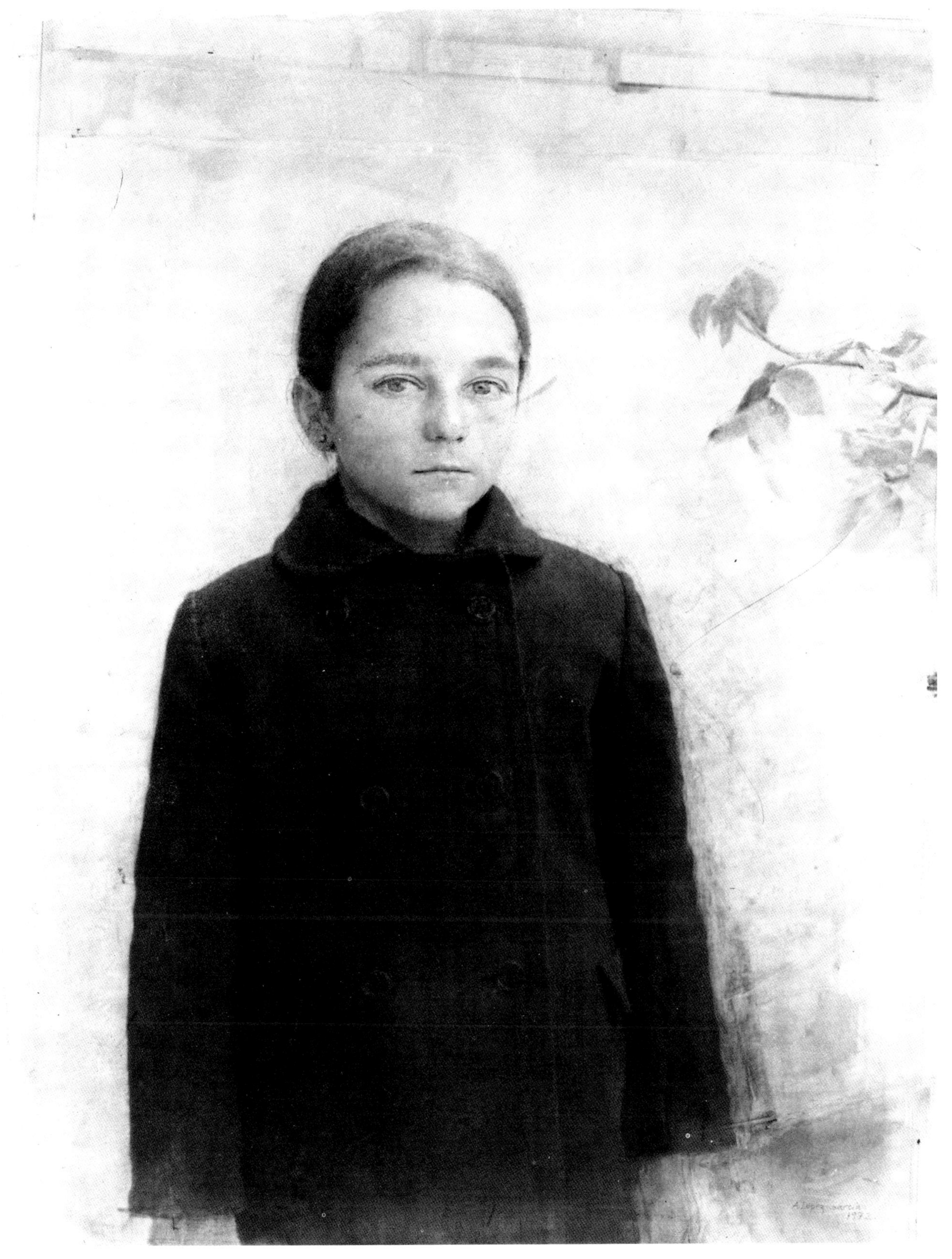

6. *María, 1972. Antonio López has always conceived draughtsmanship
as an independent technique, never an instrumental or subordinate tool.
This fact is highlighted by the relatively large format of his drawings,
in which the textures and volumes he obtains with his pencil are quite
astonishing. His gaze is particularly tender in this portrait of his elder
daughter, aged ten, depicted against the barely perceptible background
of the wall in the family garden.*

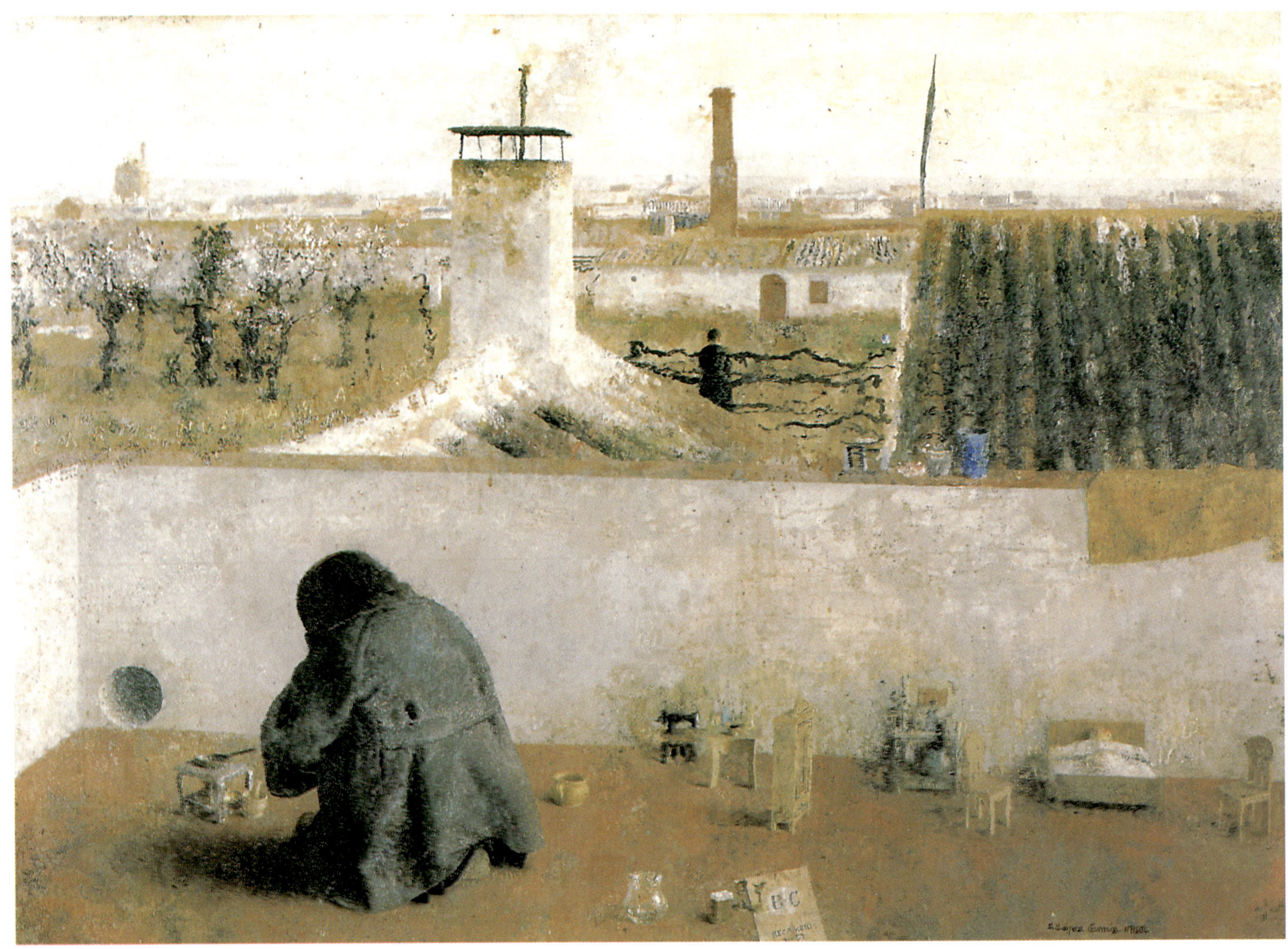

7. Carmencita Playing, 1960. The suggestive force of a figure whose back faces the viewer has been exploited by German Romantic painters such as Friedrich, and by Surrealists such as Dalí. In this picture the little girl appears engrossed in her private fantasy world of her toy furniture, elements that transform the roof terrace into a magical space that appears removed from the view of Tomelloso beyond its limits.

Memory of Tomelloso

Antonio López left his hometown for the first time in 1949 to travel to Madrid, where he began his art studies. Although he settled in Madrid in 1961, he would continue to spend time in Tomelloso, where many members of his family continue to reside. Even during the years in which he showed a greater interest in narrative and fantastic painting, the continual presence of motifs related to his birthplace reveals his deeply-rooted need to record the experiences, objects and scenarios of his life and times. Such scenes often evoke the light in the landscapes painted by his uncle and master, Antonio López Torres, under whose guidance he produced his first still lifes and vistas of the flat cultivated fields of La Mancha. Yet, above all, they provide the earliest key to his progressive tendency to unite past, present and future.

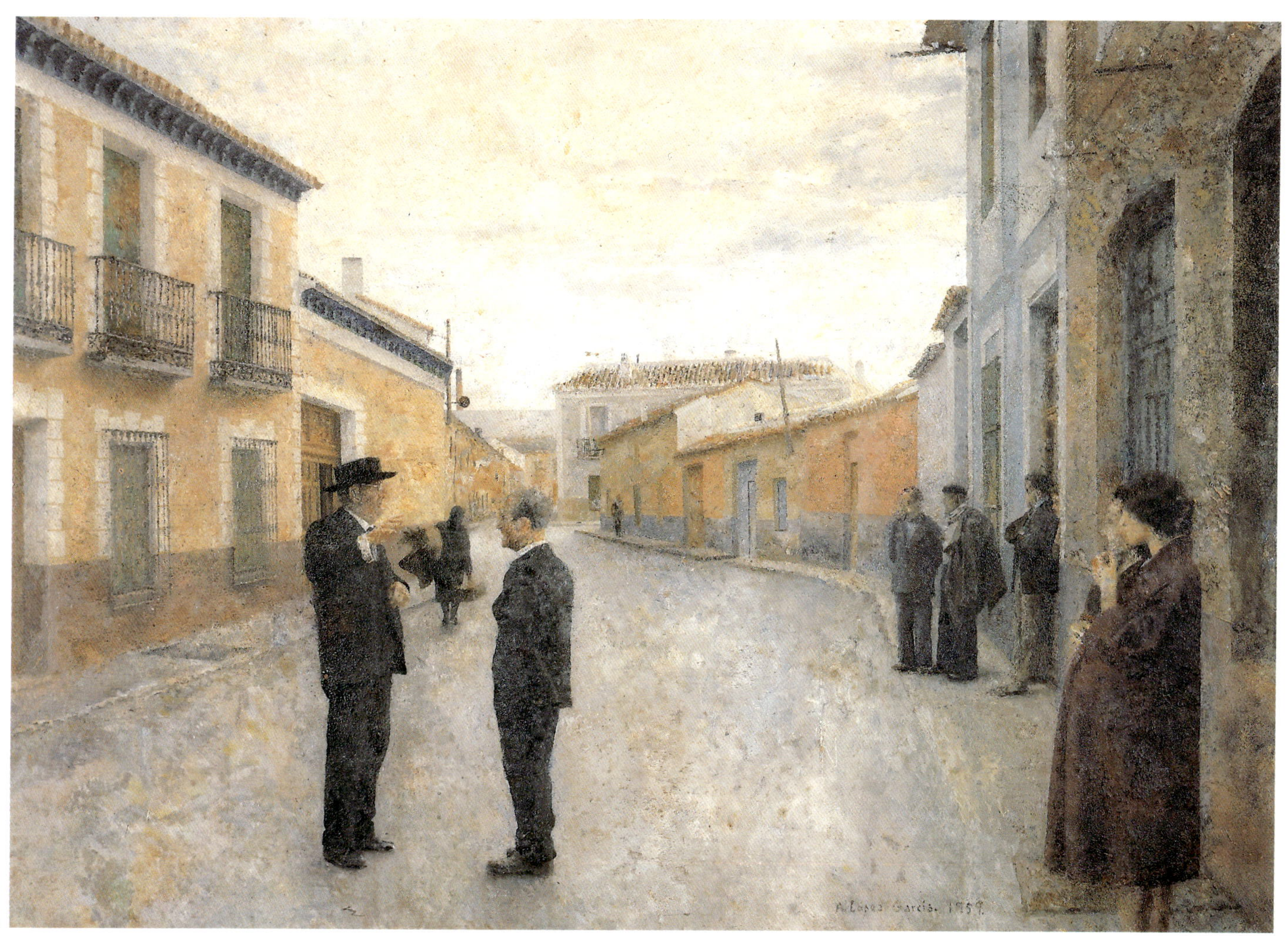

8

8. Francisco Carretero and Antonio López Torres Conversing, *1959. Francisco Carretero, a painter from Tomelloso, is depicted here in conversation with our artist's uncle and master. The other figures seem to observe their discussion, as if the two men were philosophers at the agora. Such rural scenes of village streets have a certain quality of images dreamt or conjured up from the past, and their characters take on mythical, almost archetypal airs. In the portrait of Carretero begun two years later by Antonio López the veteran painter's hand gesture matches the one portrayed here.*

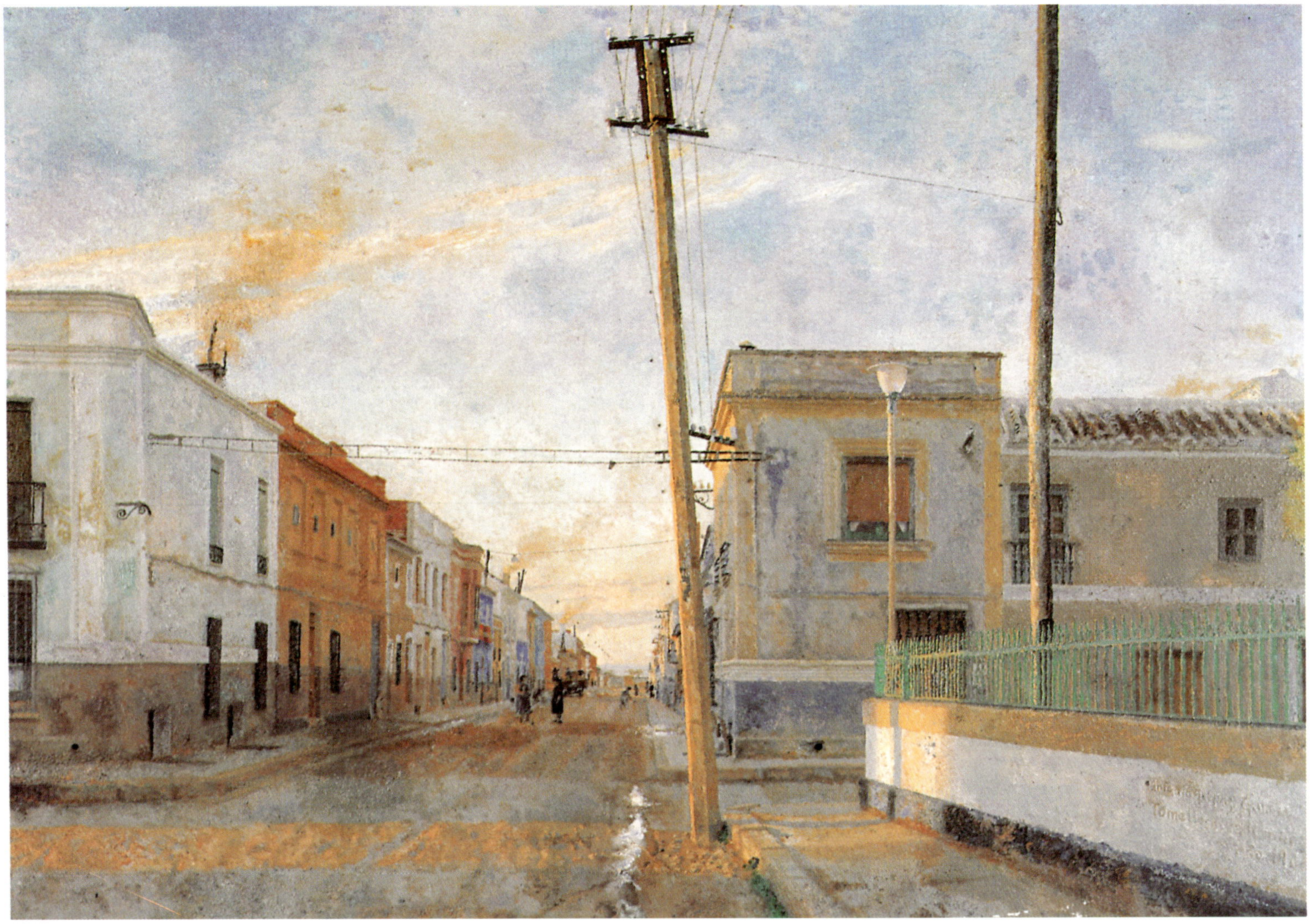

9

9. Calle Santa Rita, *1961. In contrast to
the previous work, this picture presents
a more faithful view of a street in
Tomelloso. The pictorial matter applied
by López recreates the uneven plaster of
the façades, the nuances of light on the
road surfaces and the telephone poles in
the foreground with incredible precision.*

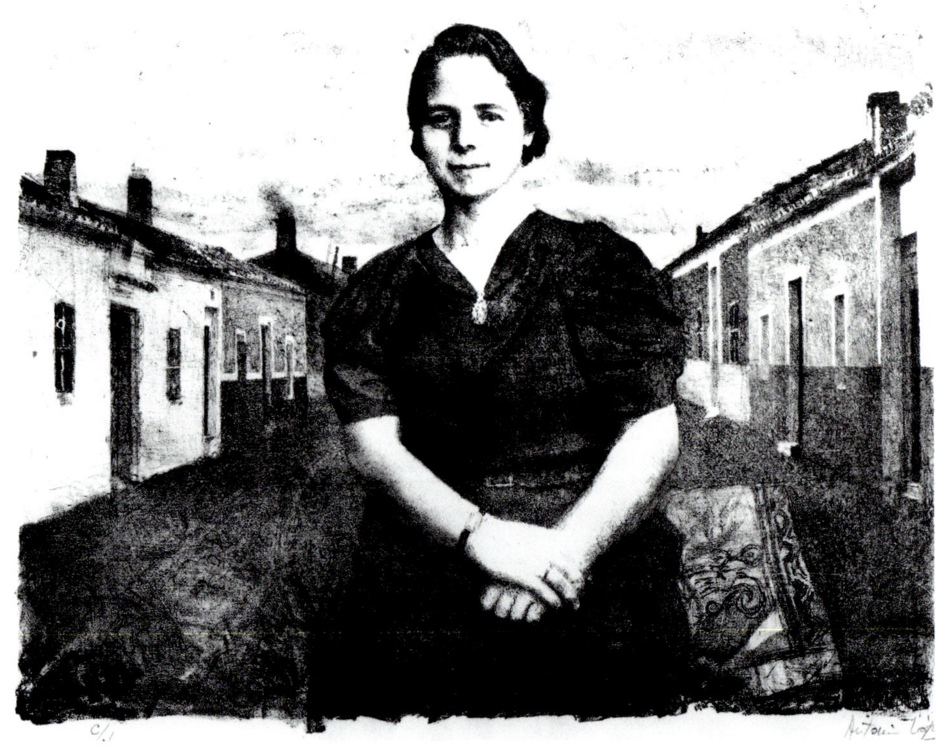

10

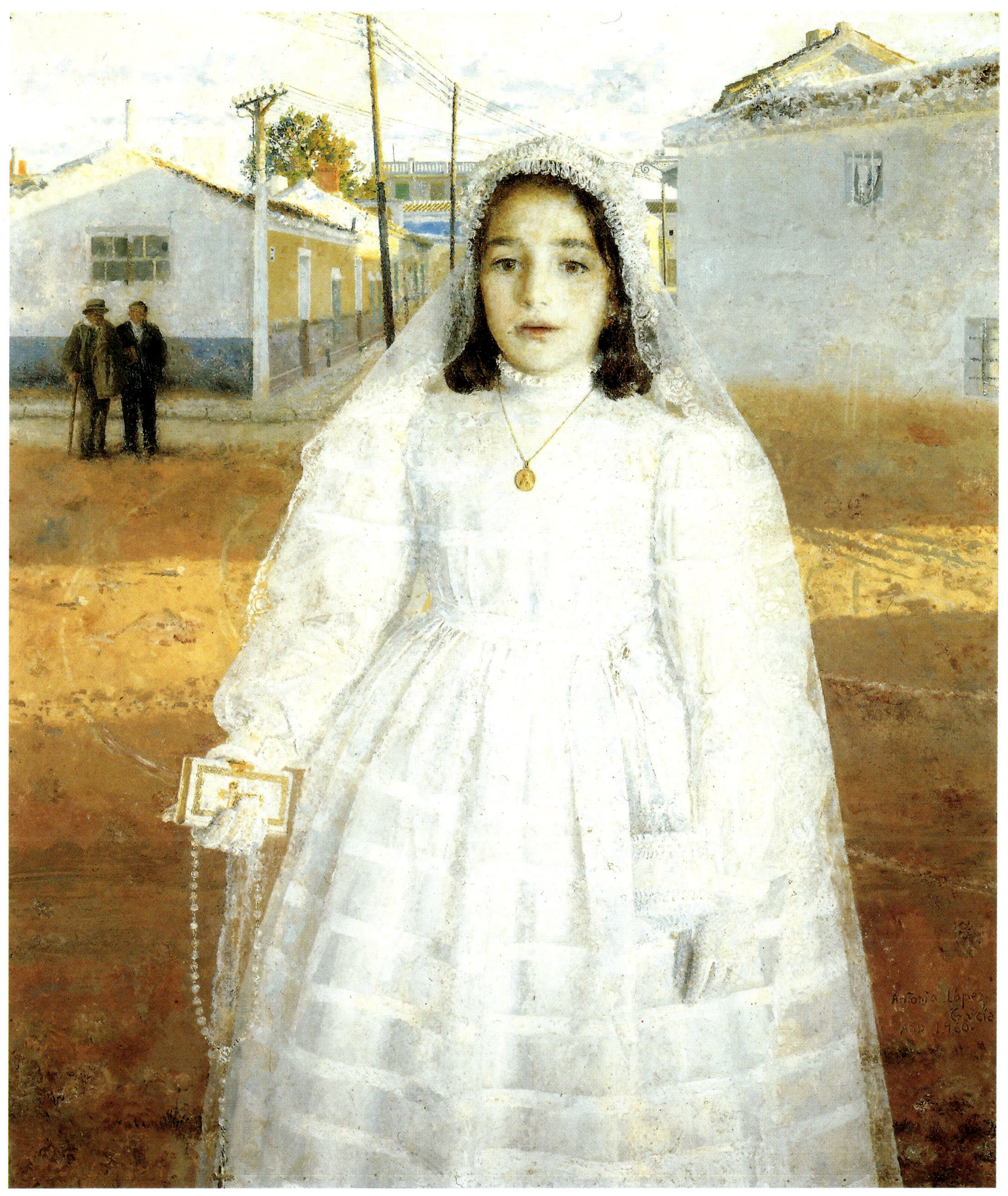

11

*10–11. Josefa, 1961. Carmencita Dressed for Holy Communion, 1960. Two unique
portraits of the painter's sisters, set against the background of Tomelloso. While
Carmencita provides yet another link to the popular iconography of those
photographs taken to immortalise family celebrations, Josefa — as if in an
allegory — seems to identify emblematically with the village, summarised by the
street represented in perspective. In the lithograph Antonio López obtains similar
qualities to those he achieves in his drawings.*

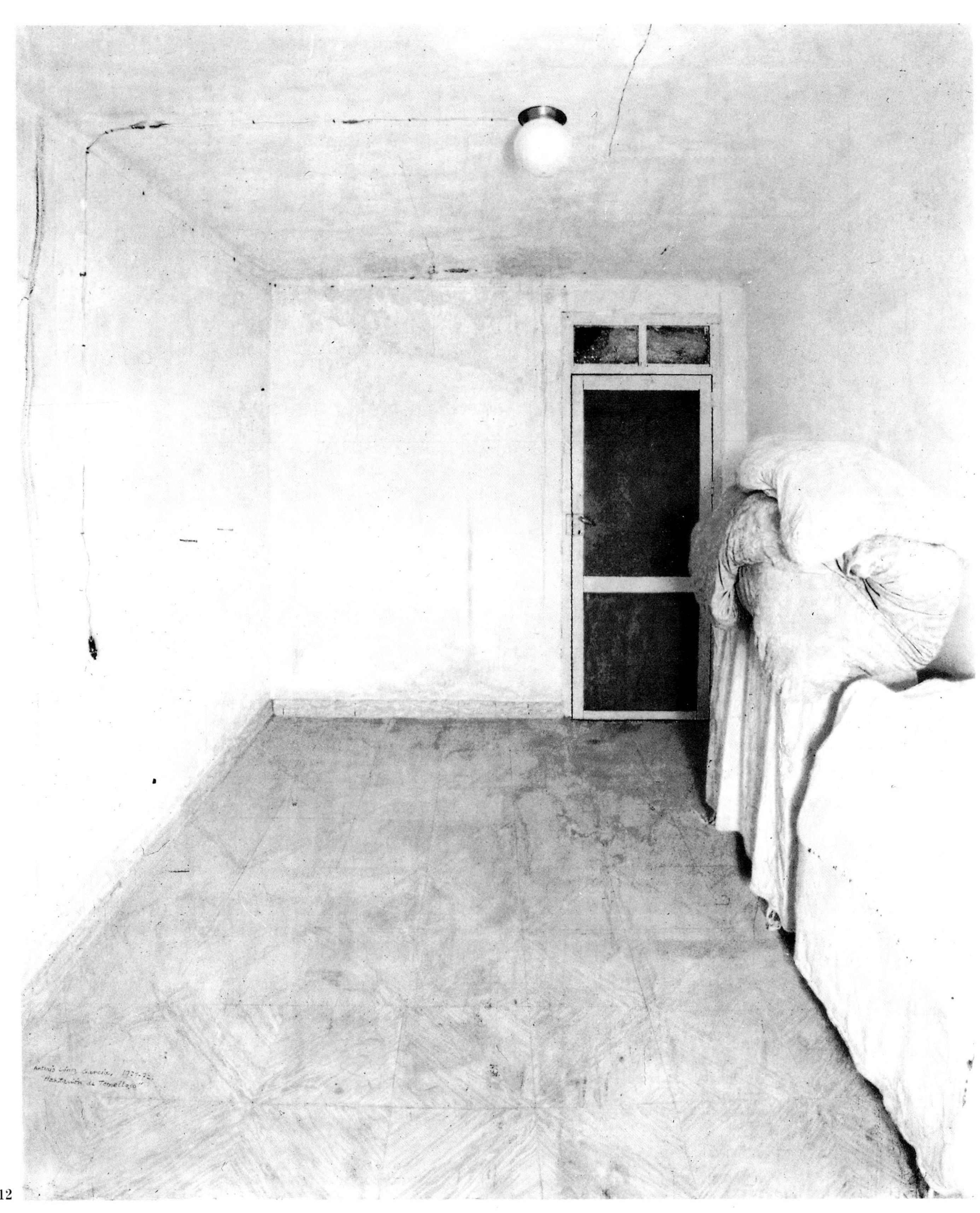

12

12. Room in Tomelloso, *1971–1972. The image of this stark room, with its items of furniture covered in dust-cloths, mysteriously evokes the presence of its past inhabitants. The damp patches and pieces of plaster that have come off the wall bear witness to the passing of time. In a similar vein, the old-fashioned light-switch hanging down the wall alongside the cable that connects it to the ceiling lamp is the very image of devastation, drawing attention to the absence of the bed that (and bed-head) that had stood there in the past.*

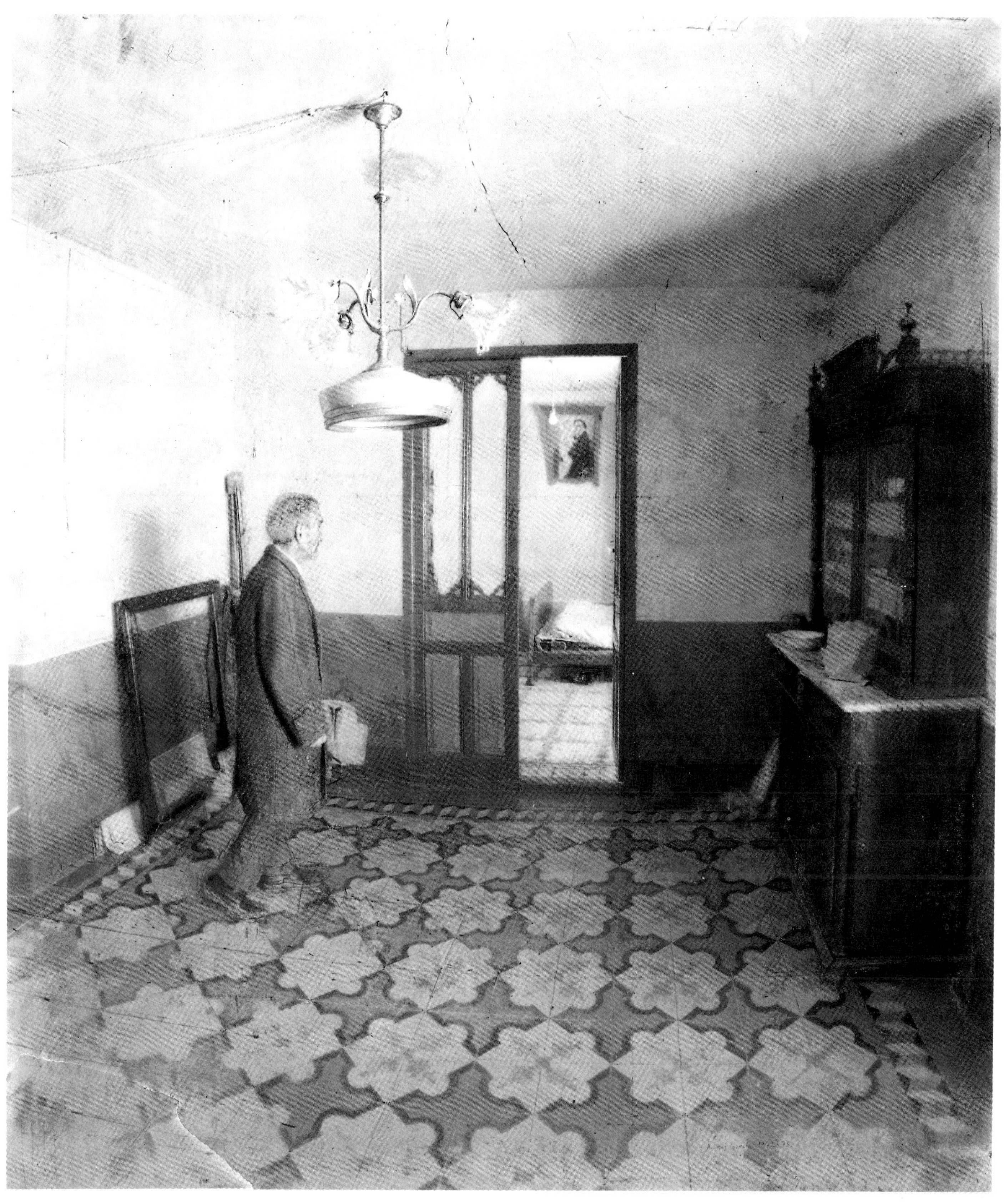

13. The House of Antonio López Torres, *1972–1975. In an existing photograph we see Antonio López indicating where his uncle should stand before setting about this drawing. The fidelity with which he has reflected not only the apparent details of this sombre interior (the lamp, pattern and texture of the terrazzo, the difference in lighting of the room in the background) but also everything they evoke (the smells, the peculiar density of the air in old houses, the unexplainable certainty that the elderly painter is the sole inhabitant of the country house) is remarkable, so much so that this scene painted from life as a tribute to his master could easily be interpreted as an oneiric vision.*

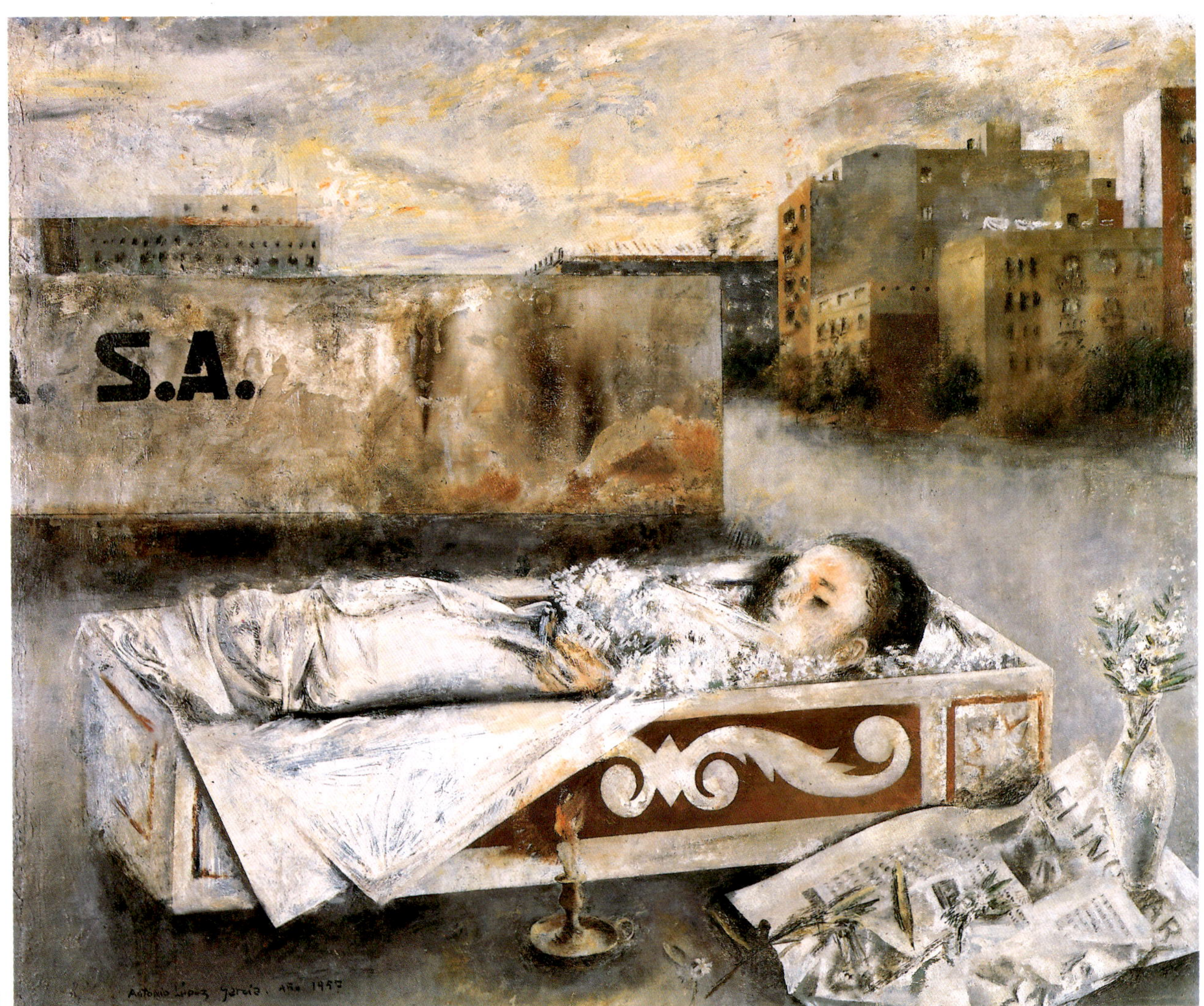

14. Dead Girl, *1957. This picture is one of those in which the presence of Surrealist ingredients is most obvious. The image of the dead child, whose relatives seem to have abandoned her during the vigil, is a metaphor of the bizarre urban environment surrounding the coffin. The industrial backdrop, anonymous and aggressive, seems to be the place of lost hopes, clearly symbolised by the little girl's premature death.*

On the Verge of Reality

Critics used the term Magic Realism to describe the most significant works produced by Antonio López between the late fifties and the mid sixties. It referred to the increasing faithfulness with which the artist depicted objects and spaces, combined with a Surrealist taste for conflicting associations of images and their de-contextualisation. Appraising this period in retrospect, it takes on different connotations — somehow these paintings seem to seek hidden meanings in perceived reality, suggesting the presence of a mysterious perspective crucially explored by the artist, a presence he will never surrender, merely approach in an increasingly direct fashion over the course of time. He had begun by attempting to depict the ghosts veiled by reality, and would proceed to interpret reality itself as a ghost, an elusive phenomenon he strove to secure in his canvases. Strangely enough, Antonio López may stray from fantasy, but mystery merely becomes deeper and more disturbing.

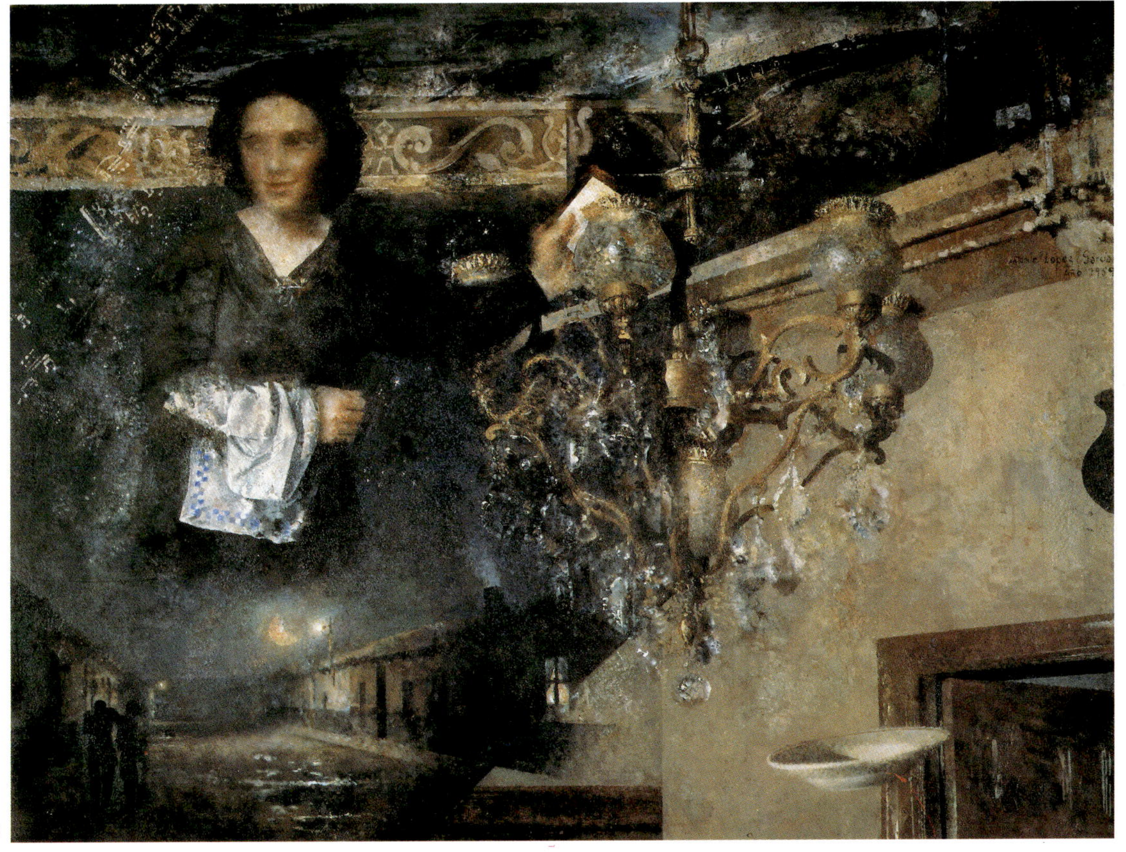

15

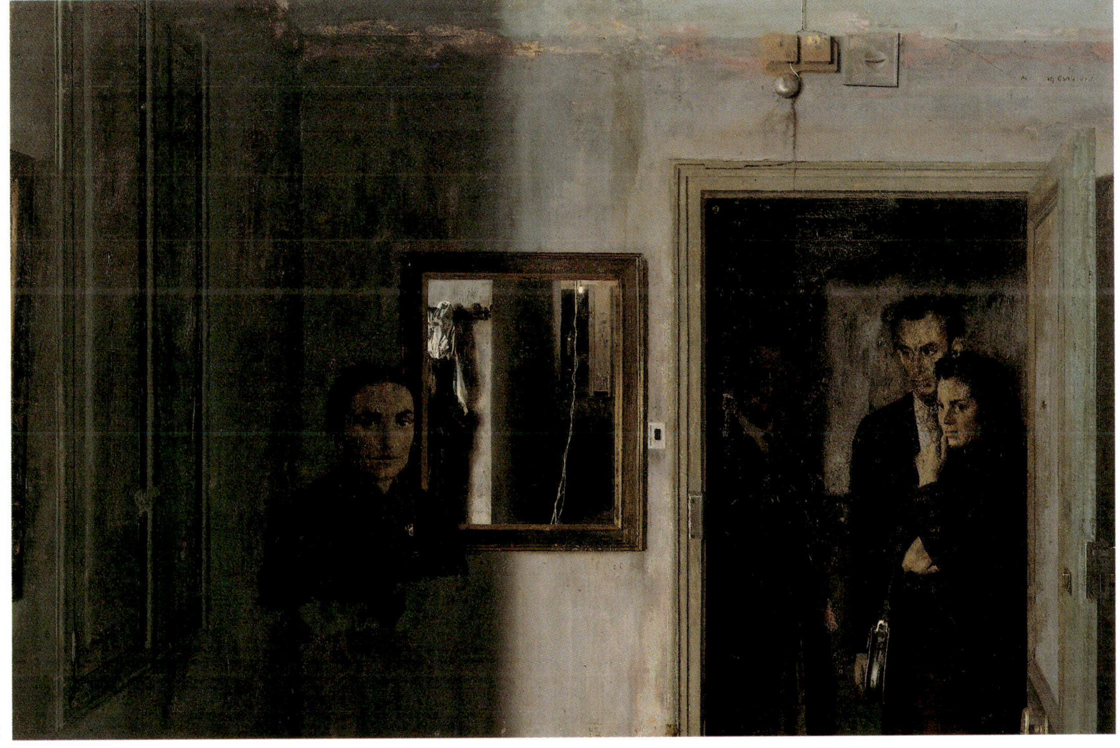

16

15–16. The Lamp, *1959.*
Figures in a House, *1967.*
*These two works reveal the
progressive refinement of the
Surrealist resources in the
oeuvre of Antonio López. In
the first picture we observe a
combination of interior and
exterior that seems to follow
in the wake of Magritte,
with figures floating in the
imprecise realm structured
around a set of meaningful
associations — the moon and
the chandelier, the dark of
night and the presence of light.
The second picture, which can
be interpreted as a fantastic
though perhaps unfinished
work, is a painstakingly
painted interior peopled by
dubious presences (the trio
standing in the doorway),
and by another that appears
to be vanishing before our
very eyes (the female figure
in the foreground). The space,
doorway and mirror seem
to evoke Velázquez'* The Maids
of Honour.

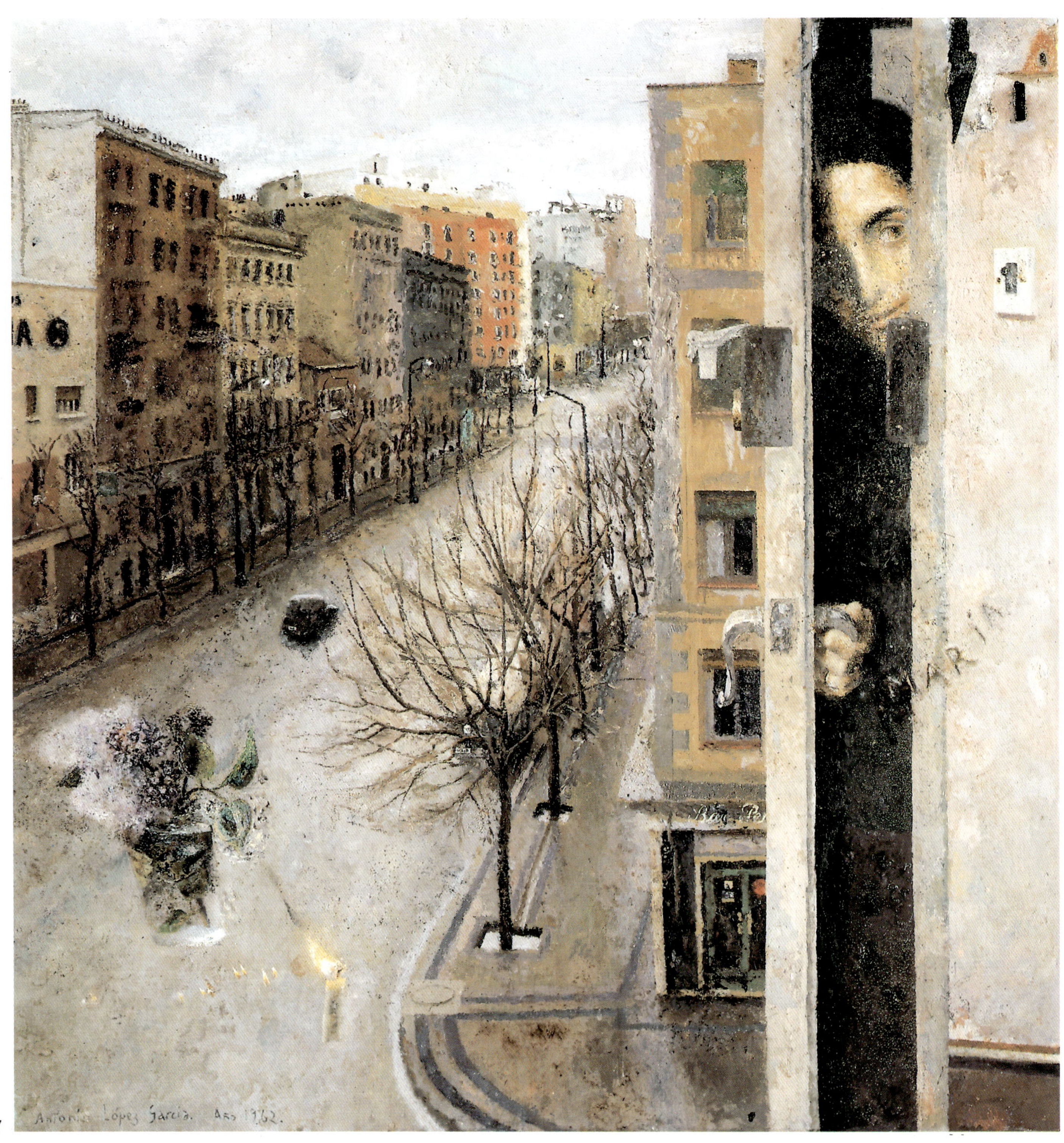

17. Mari in the Embajadores Neighbourhood, *1962. Following his marriage and decision to settle in Madrid in 1961 Antonio López lived in this neighbourhood for a short period of time. This painting preserves a certain number of Surrealist touches, such as the paradoxical relationship between interior and exterior, the candle and the vase of flowers floating in space, and yet it is also reveals his interest in cityscapes. The tendency to simplify and synthesise the formal elements of the painter's early years is still present, as is the unmistakable material texture of his surfaces.*

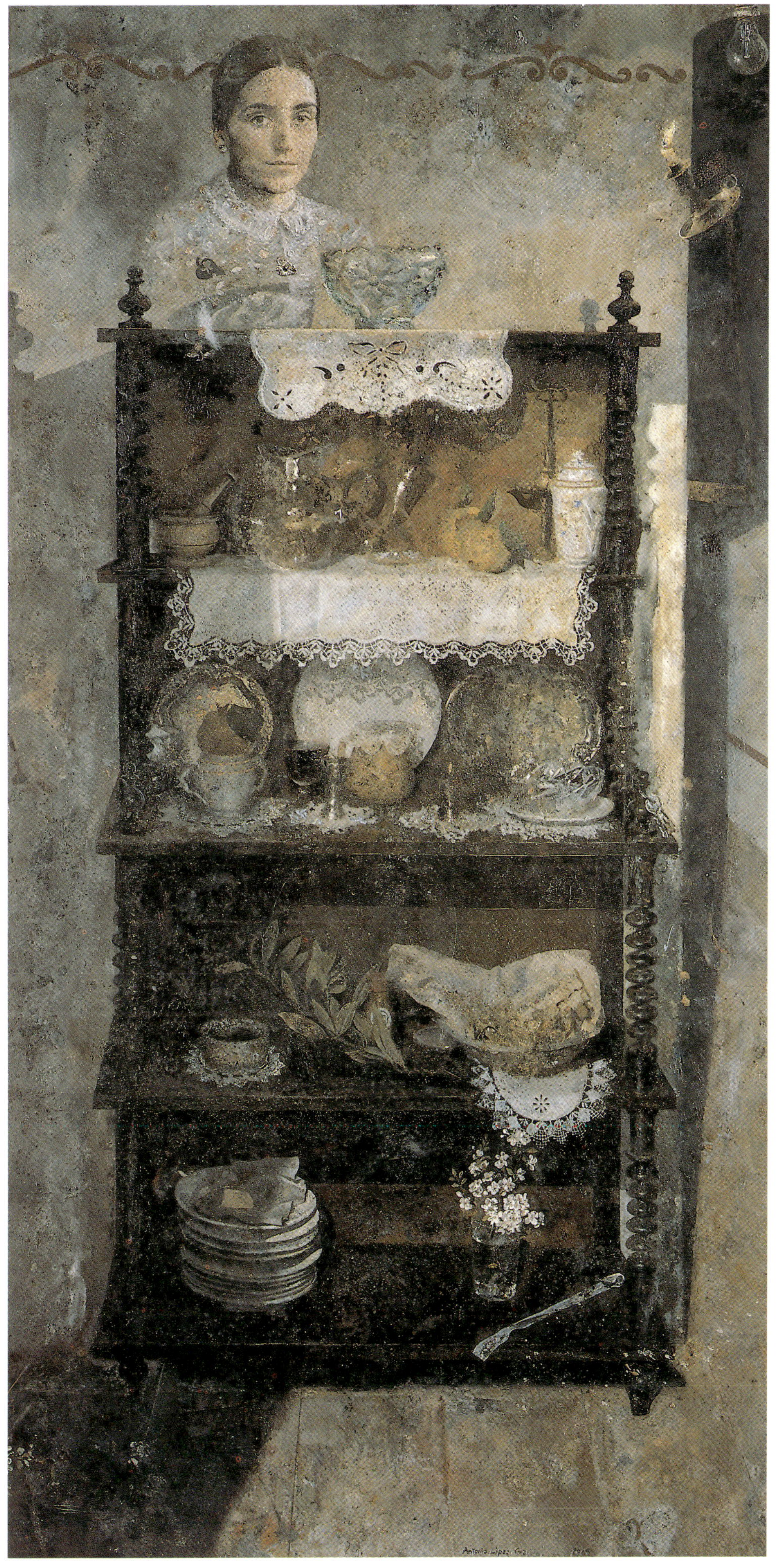

18. The Dresser, *1963. As in* Figures in a House, *painted four years later, in this work Antonio López introduces an evanescent figure, almost an apparition. Again, we come across the depiction of a candle floating in space, which on this occasion is related to the light bulb depicted in the upper right-hand corner. The changes in the painter's approach to his motifs can be clearly traced if we compare this picture to* The China Cabinet, *painted between 1965 and 1966.*

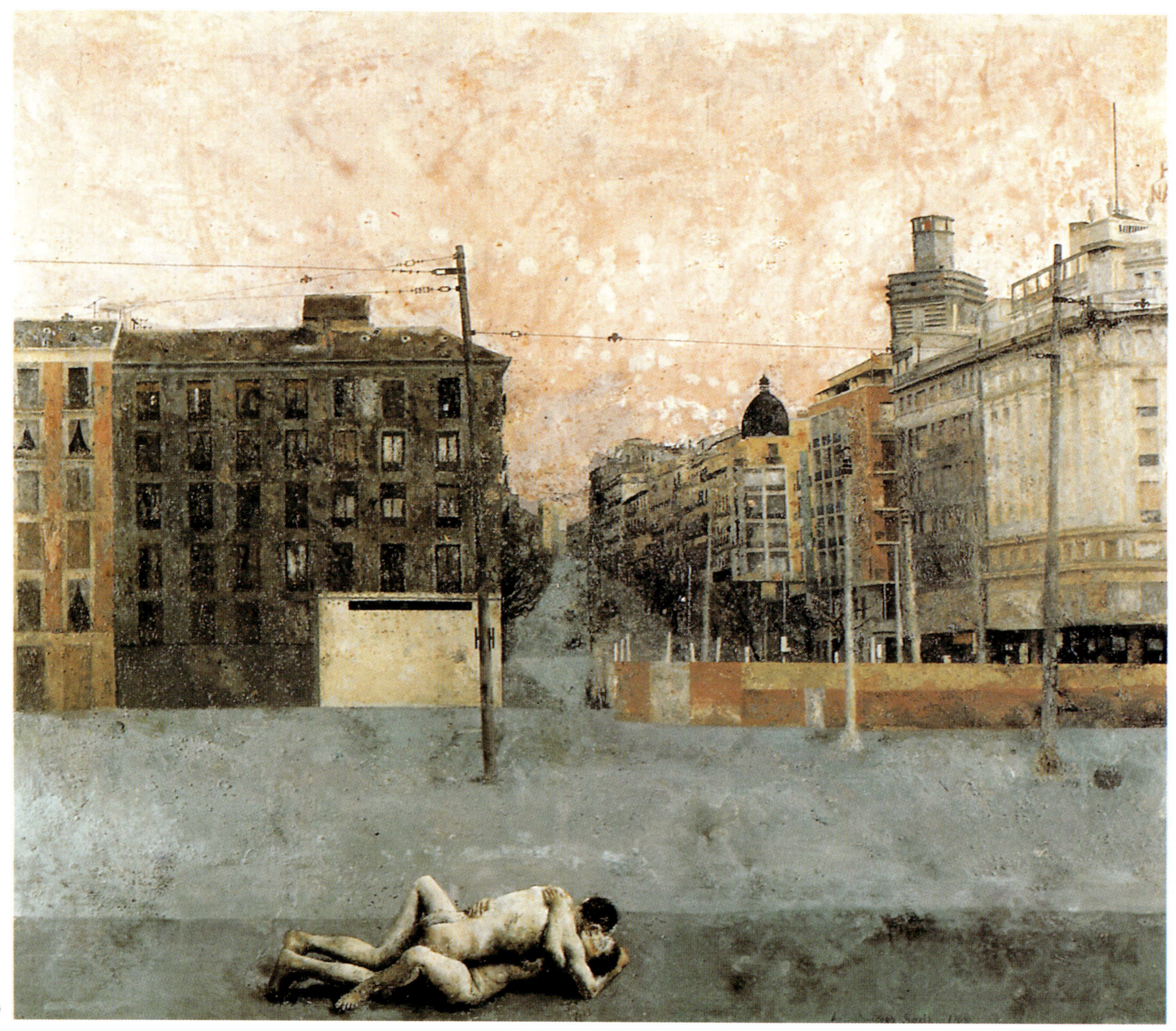

19. Atocha, *1964. Some critics, such as Giovanni Testori, have interpreted this work as the counterpart to* Dead Girl, *of 1957. While in the earlier picture the city was the setting of death and lost hopes, here it is associated with the act of copulation that creates life. In 1964 Antonio López lived at Embajadores, a district close to the Atocha roundabout and railway station, so this scene could well be a recreation of his first view of the city upon his first arrival.*

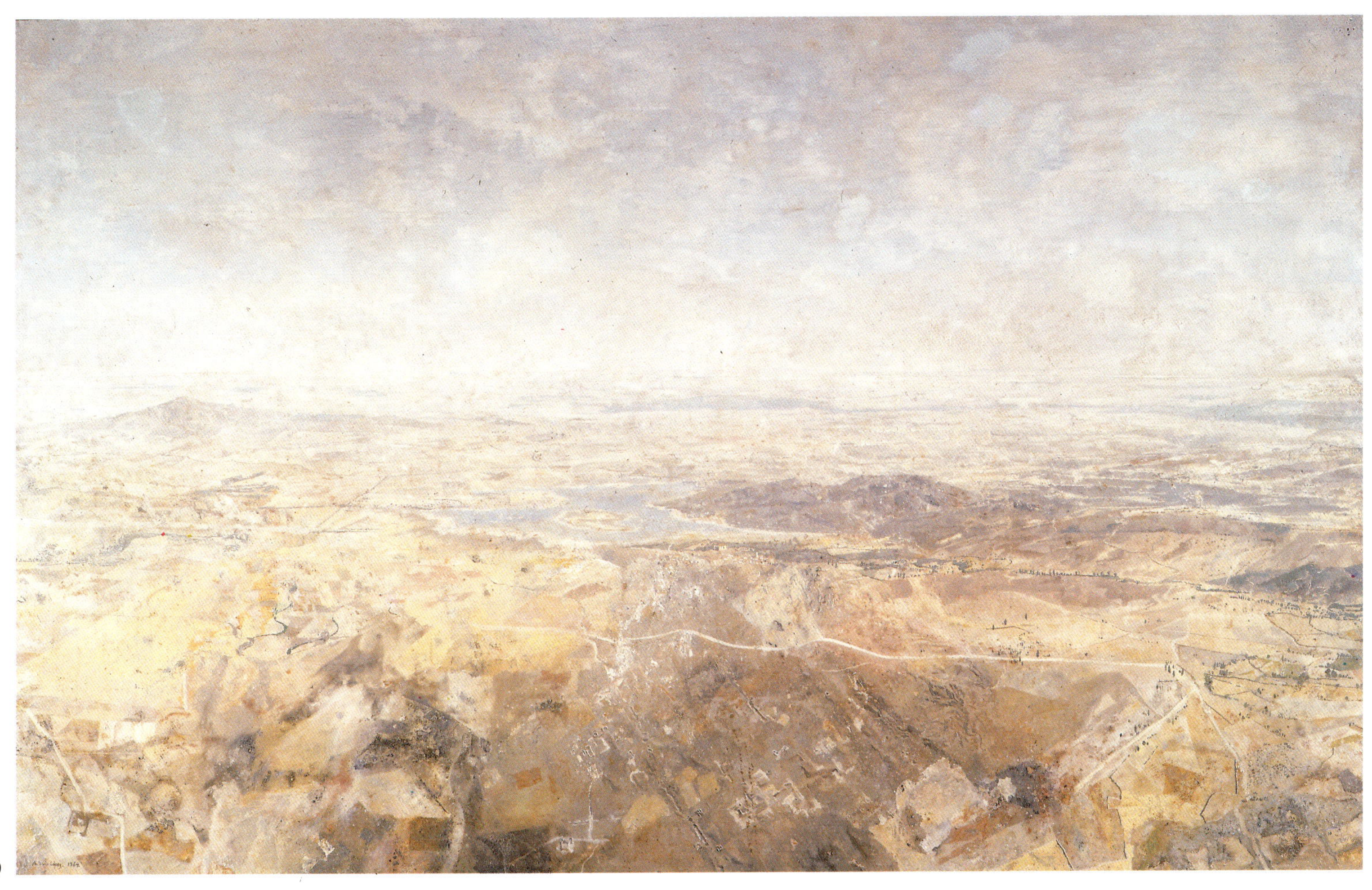

20. North Madrid Seen from "La Maliciosa", *1964. La Maliciosa is one of the peaks of the Guadarrama mountain range, near Madrid. In 1962 Antonio López went hiking there, taking advantage of the fact that he was spending the summer in a nearby village. As the artist has told Michael Brenson, "The whole plain of north Madrid could be seen, miles and miles of golden soil under the summer sun. It was so wonderful that I picked up a board measuring six feet by three feet and started to paint it." This is one of the few occasions on which Antonio López decides to paint something he has just seen, which affords the composition an unreal poetic air, in spite of the almost topographical fidelity with which he renders the motif. The delicate nuances of light and the precise gradation of pictorial matter relate this vista to some of his subsequent cityscapes.*

Objects
and Images

Antonio López has stated that "Man has always sought to understand the experience of other human beings through vision." This possibility of sharing our gaze with others is one of the few certainties on which the Castilian painter bases his Realism, a shred of that ontological unity of the real on which the Naturalism of the old masters was established. By rendering a specific motif in painting, the artist somehow yields his gaze to the viewer. As Antonio López himself says apropos Vermeer, "the eyes of the beholder are seemingly the eyes of Vermeer contemplating the scene, and yet we know that it is a painting, an convention ruled by intricate laws pervaded by his spirit." In the work of Antonio López this duality is expressed in the obvious marks that his struggle with the motif has left on the pictorial surface (compared, not in vain, to a layer of skin) in the form of traces of matter flanking other unfinished areas. The tension between objects and their painted images evinces the radical modernism of his Realism, derived from a conflicting and rigorous notion of reality.

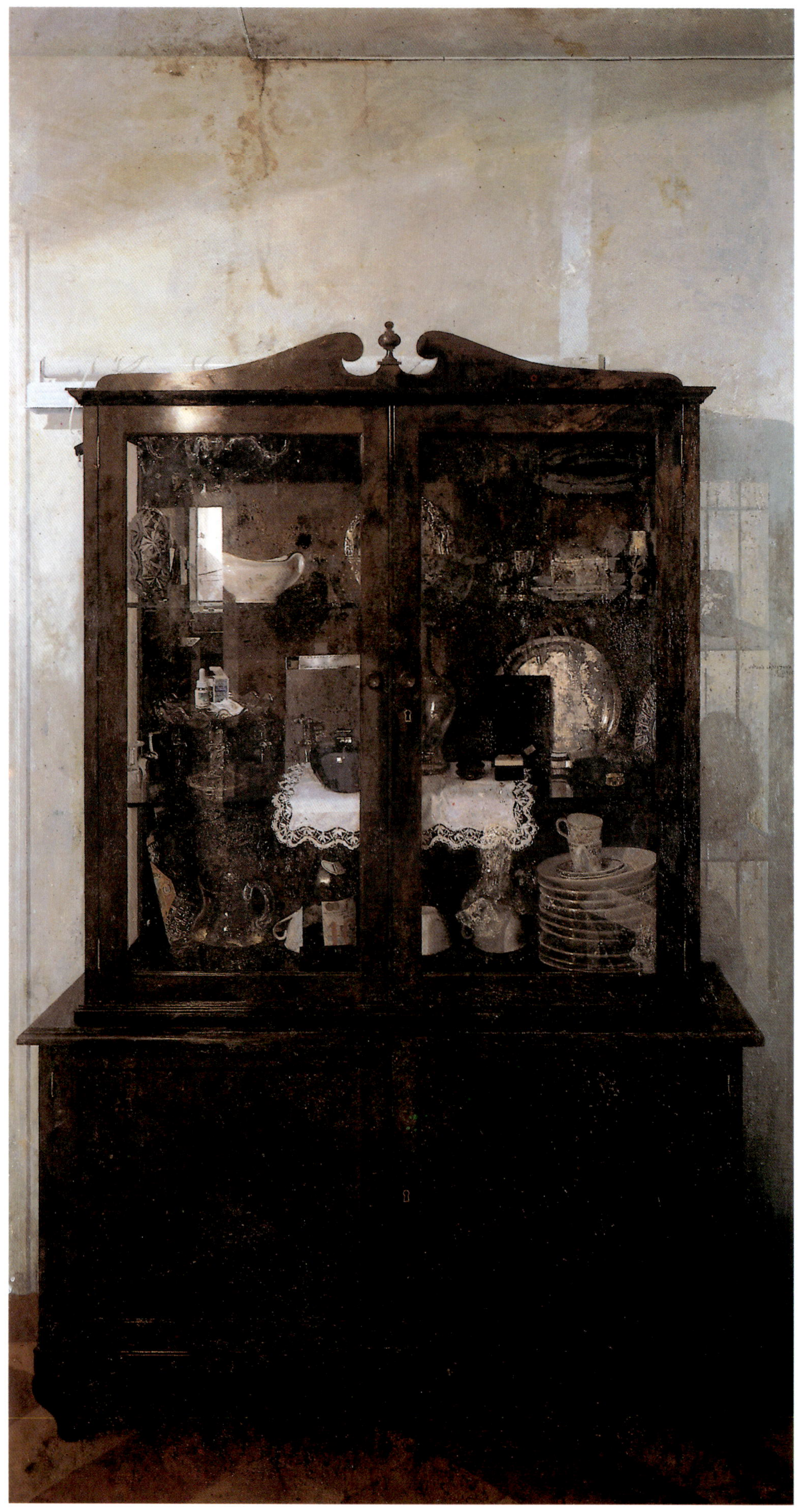

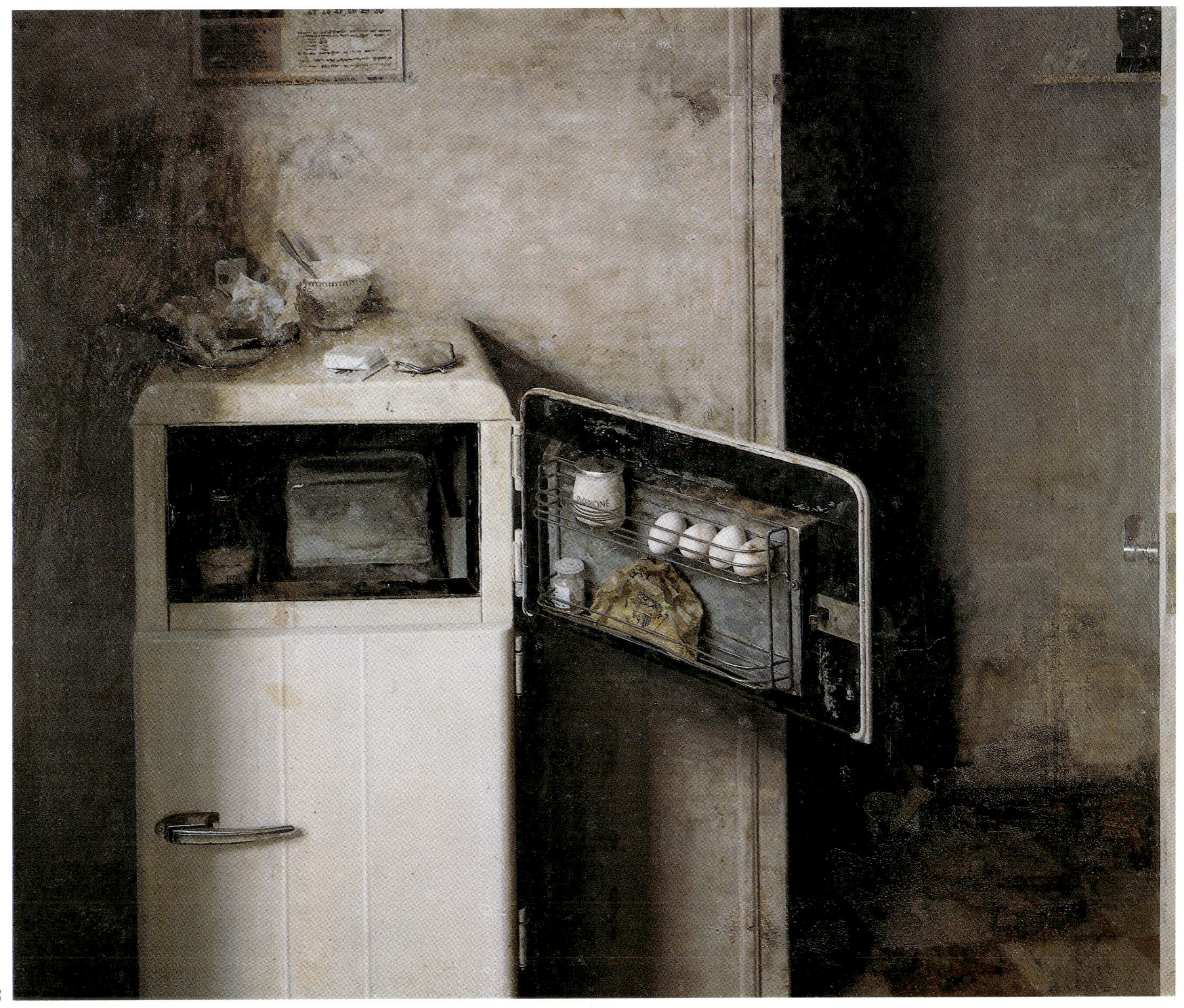

21. The China Cabinet, *1965–1966. In comparison with* The Dresser *of 1962, the artist's approach to pictorial motifs in this painting is significantly different. While the characteristic feature of the previous work has disappeared — the translucent veil that seemed to come between the picture and the beholder — some of the uncertainty still remains, this time stemming from the precision of the artist's gaze, from the way in which the china dinner service seems to overlap the light reflected from the window on to the glass door of the cabinet, and from the powerful rendering of the various different textures and shiny surfaces.*

22. Icebox, *1966. Antonio López is a keen observer of his surroundings (his own house and the everyday objects it contains), as proven by his recreations of these domestic interiors. This choice of subject matter is a way of jolting collective memory, given that over the course of time such ordinary motifs often acquire a rare quality, unfamiliar to some and practically forgotten by many. In both cases the most outstanding features are the traces of time and memory.*

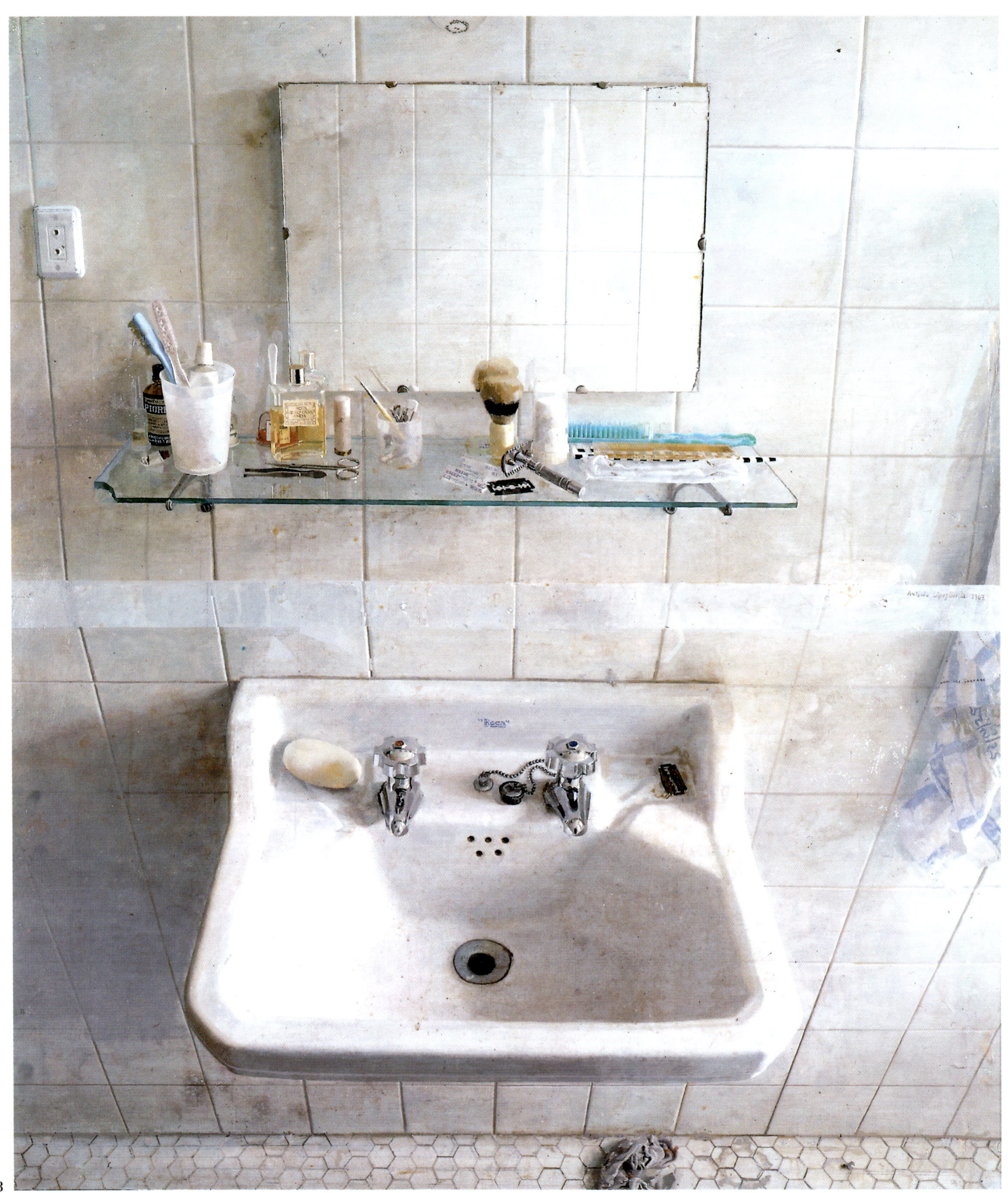

23

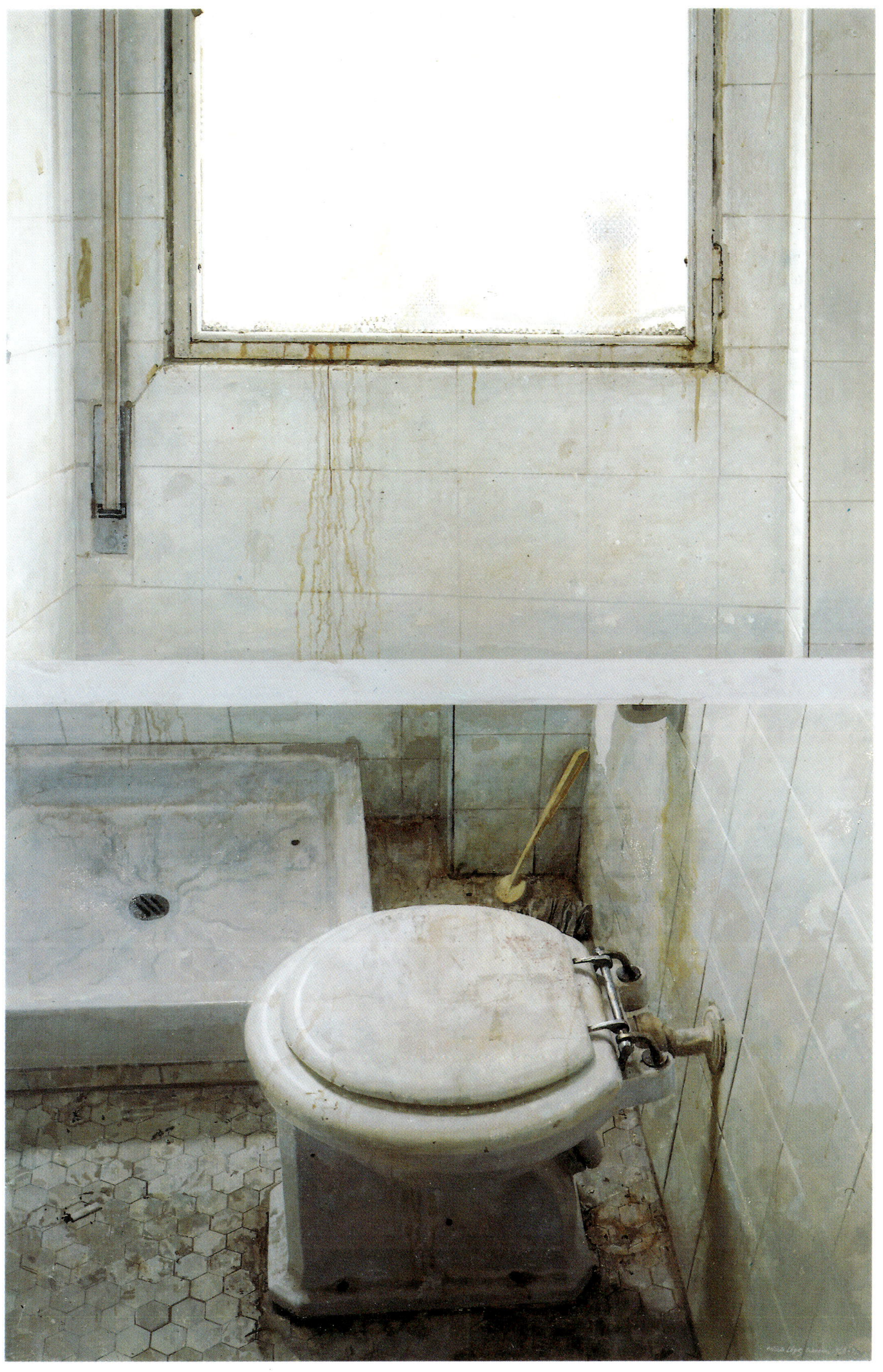

23–24. Hand Basin and Mirror, *1967.* Lavatory Pan and Window, *1968–1971. The initial reactions of viewers before these two works are surprise at such uncommon motifs and admiration of the painstaking recreation of details. In both cases the bright smooth texture of the tiles called for a homogeneous application of paint. Another common feature is the existence of two different perspectives in each composition, emphasised by the presence of a wide horizontal band indicating the two-dimensional nature of the works.*

24

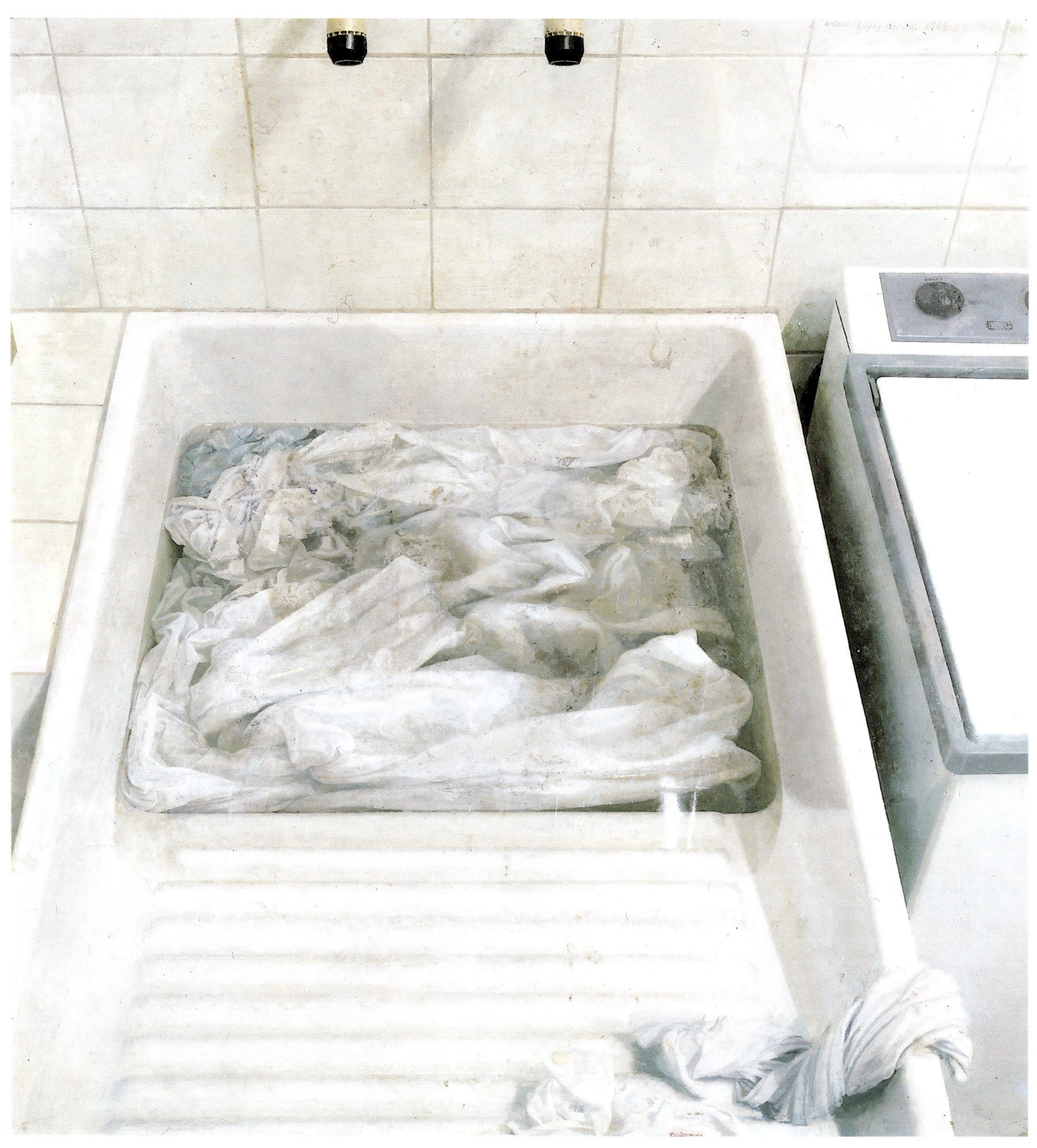

25

25. Clothes in Soak, *1968. This absolutely trivial image
is intensified by the extreme proximity and height of
the angle from which it has been painted, reproducing
the gaze of someone standing in front of the sink. The
fragmentary quality of the composition is patently clear
in the forced oblique view of the washing machine on the
right and the nozzles of the taps above. The position of
each element on the picture plane creates visual tension
between the superficial quality of the painted image and
the realistic virtuosity of the light, shade and reflections
on the tiled wall.*

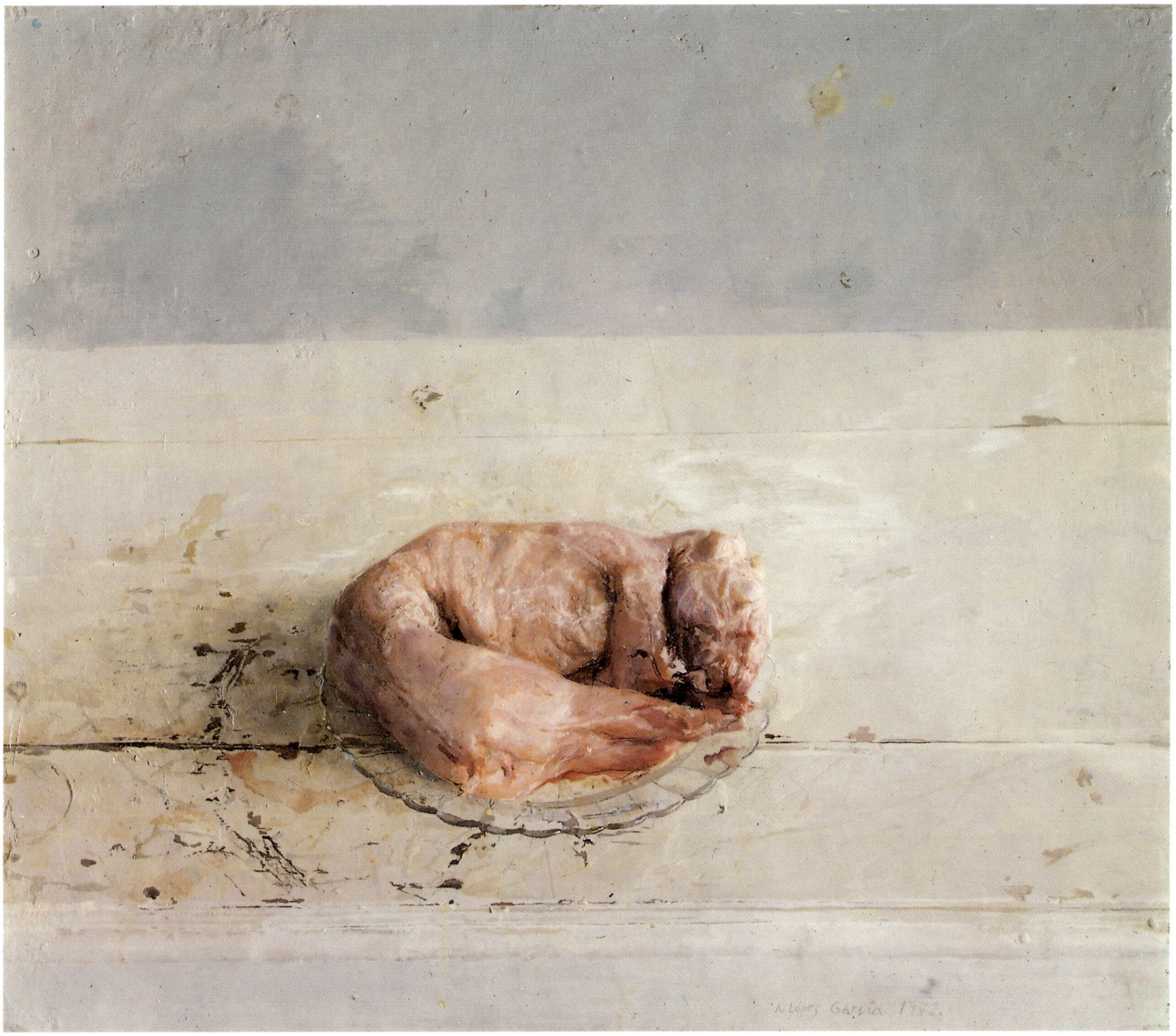

26

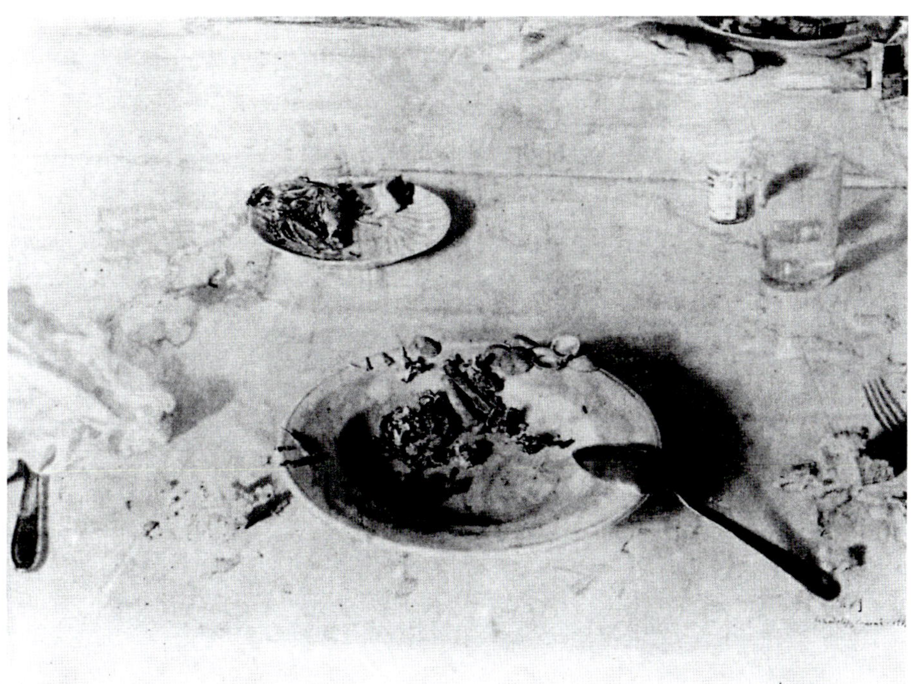

27

26–27. *Skinned Rabbit, 1972.*
Leftovers, 1971. Two further works
in which the extraordinarily precise
rendering of unexpected motifs seen
from very close range charges them
with special intensity. The subject
matter of both compositions recalls
some of the most emblematic
paintings by Dalí, who was
especially attracted to such themes.
The somewhat ambiguous spatial
relationships between the dish and
the shelf on which it stands in
Skinned Rabbit *also evokes certain*
Spanish still lifes of the seventeenth
century, although such distortions
are quite frequent features in López'
oeuvre.

City and Time

The vistas of Madrid, begun in 1960, are perhaps the most well known works by Antonio López. They are large-scale compositions, chiefly horizontal and painstakingly executed *en plein air* over extended periods of time. They are the best example of what Calvo Serraller calls "a truly borderline attempt to blend the temporality of the subject matter into both pictorial and psychological time," vital for the understanding of the Castilian artist's oeuvre. The city (the stage of modern life *par excellence*) is a true model of reality — a permanent structure in its streets and buildings, yet a changing polymorphous configuration as well. The painter always sets about his task in the present, a present that expands during the long periods of execution, and is concentrated in specific hours and lighting conditions, those in which he actually paints. Much has been written on the barenness of his deserted streets, but in point of fact this is only the result of the painter's need to dismiss all that which cannot be captured by his arrested gaze, at once dramatically eternal and fleeting.

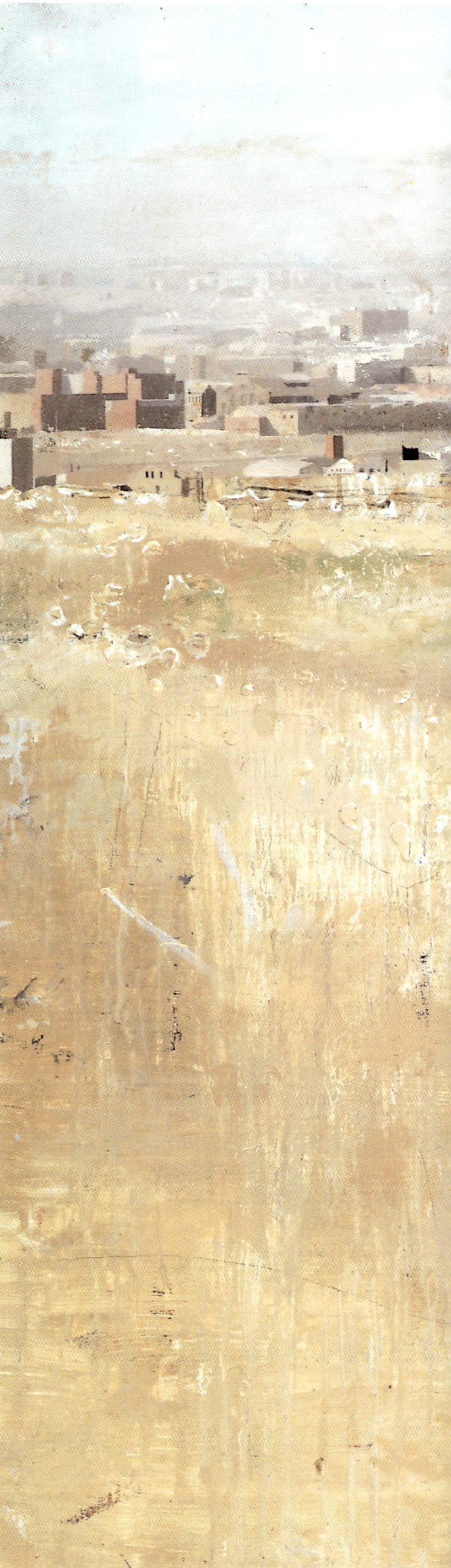

28. Madrid Seen from Tío Pío Hill, 1962–1963. This is one of the artist's first panoramic views of Madrid, painted from a high point located south of the city. The buildings appear in the distance, translated into small, juxtaposed planes of light and shade. More than half the composition depicts the stretch of land that stands between the position occupied by the painter and the cityscape, an expanse rendered in a style verging on Art Informel, *drippings included — the memory of Goya's* The Dog *comes instantly to mind. However, the two halves are united by a meticulous gradation of light ranging from the golden tones of the foreground to the blue hues of the sky, which is cut short in the distance.*

28

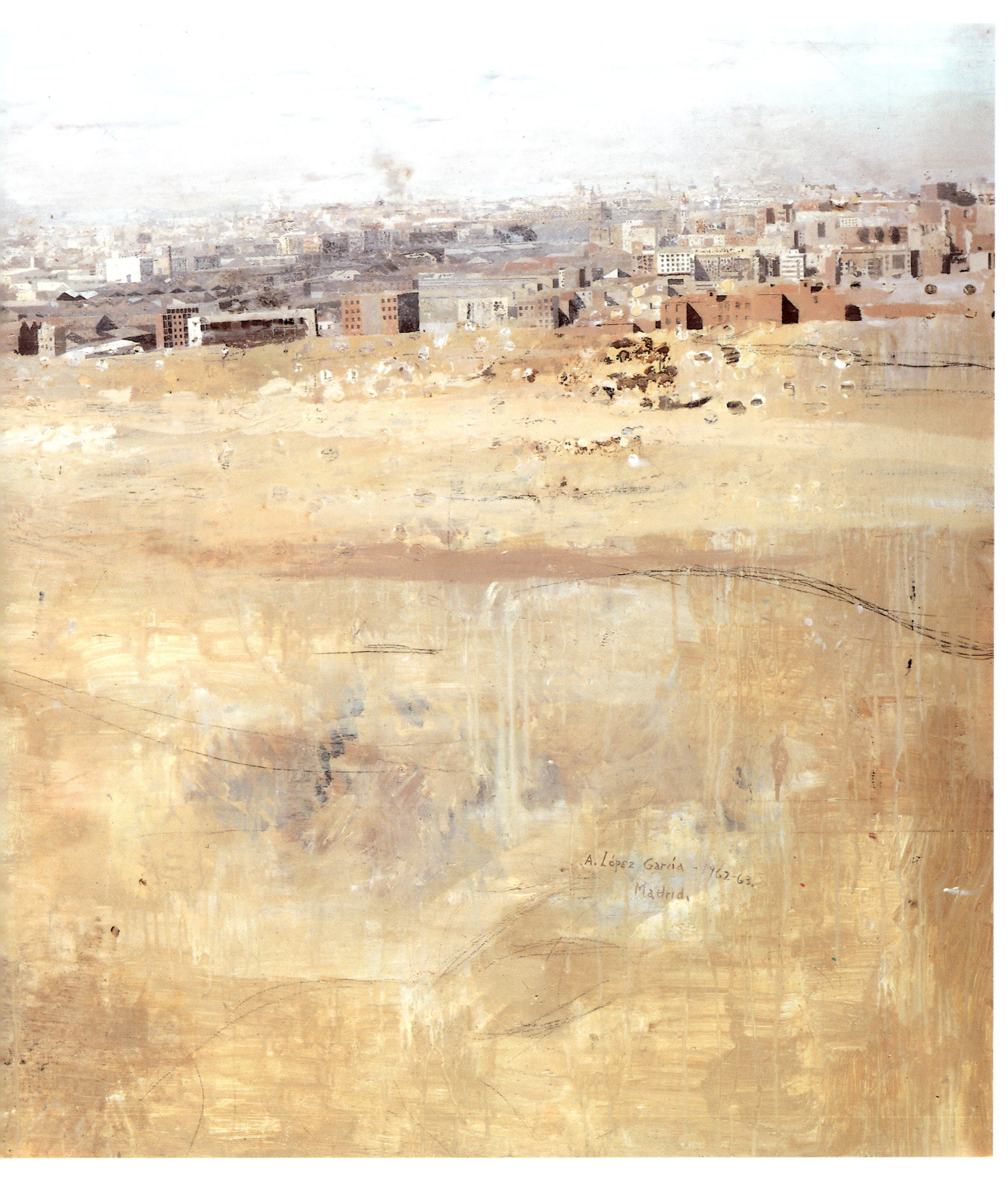

A. López García - 1962-63.
Madrid.

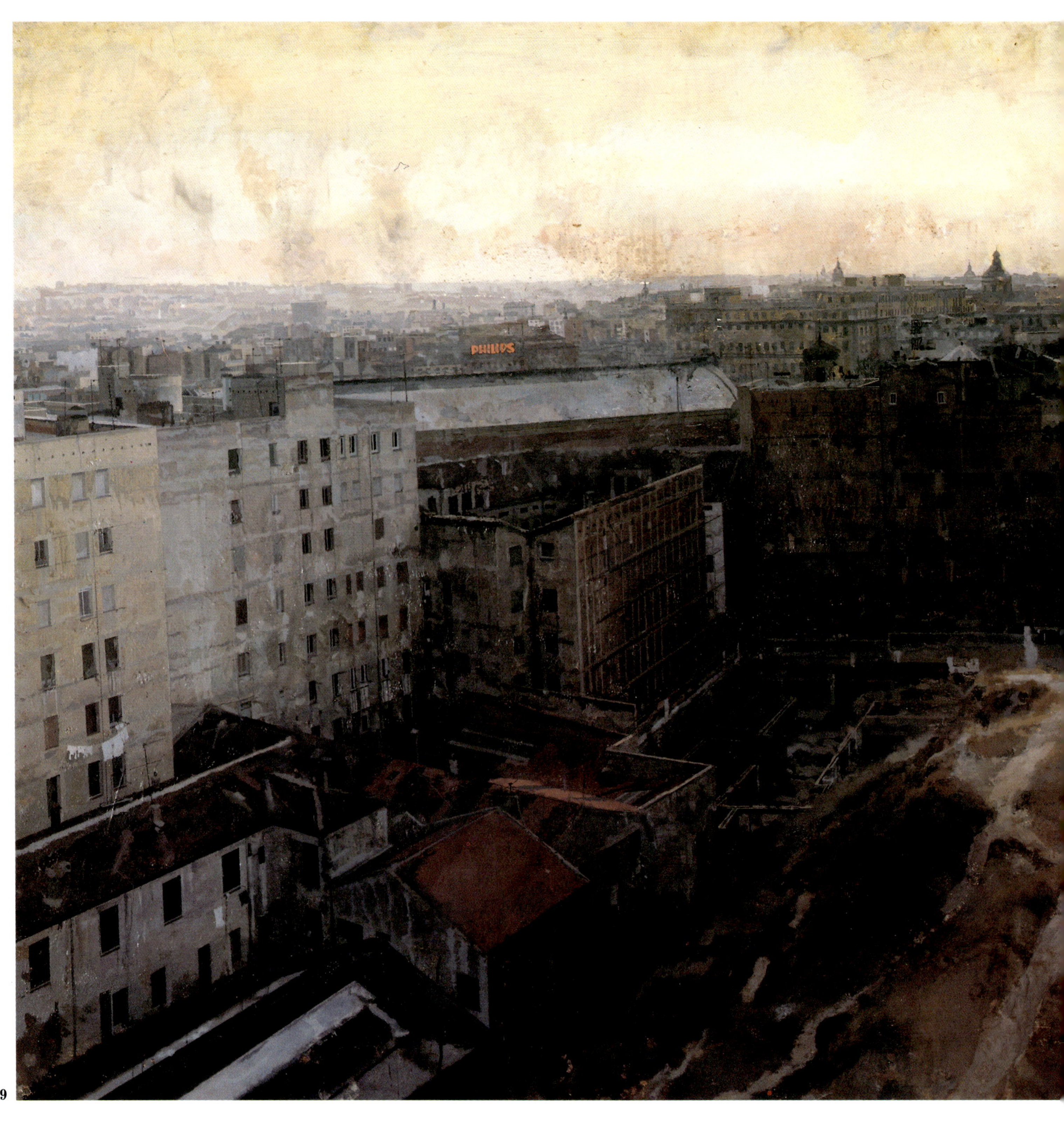

29

29. Madrid Looking towards the Observatory, *1965–1970. Painted from San Blas hill, the site of the Astronomical Observatory (the circular construction on the right), this vista opens out towards the southwest of the city. In the foreground we see the party walls and rear façades of the buildings that look onto* paseo Infanta Isabel, calle Alfonso XII *and a building still under construction. The latter is an explicit reference to the idea of the city as a living organism in constant change, modified over the course of time. Antonio López usually prefers to paint such views at dawn or dusk, when the light presents a wider range of subtle nuances.*

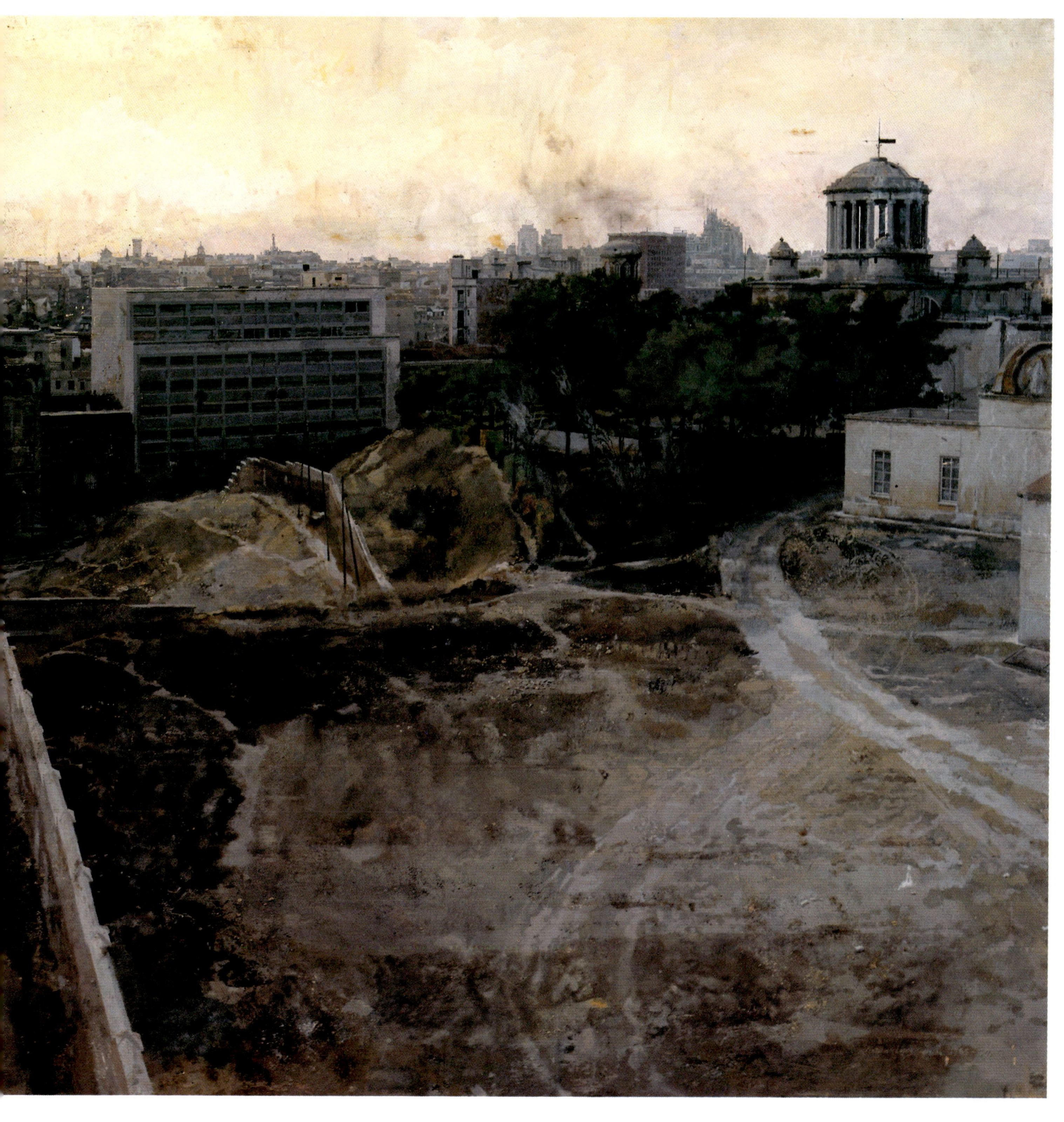

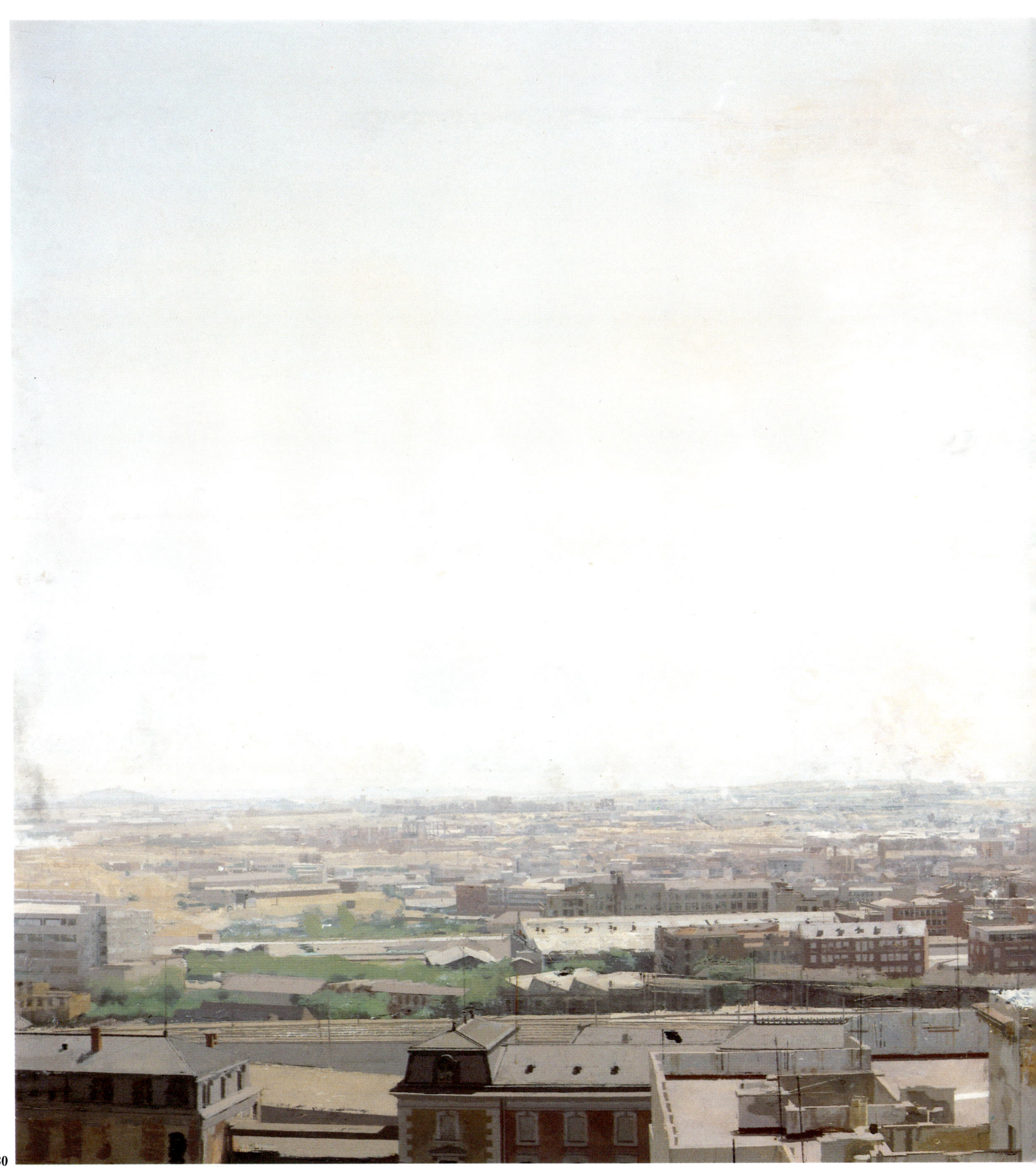

30

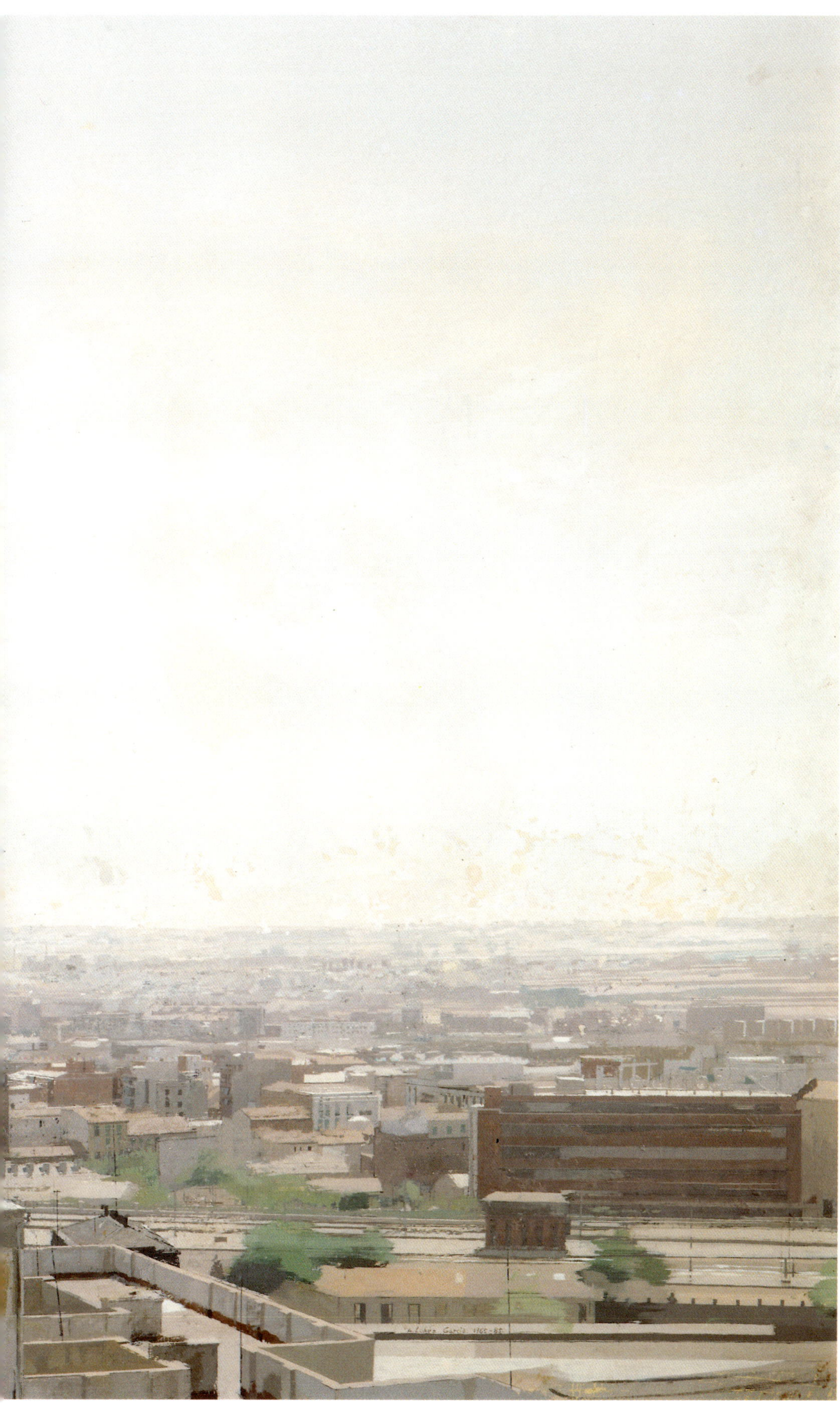

30. South Madrid, *1965–1985.*
If the previous picture presented
a panoramic view of Madrid's
old quarter, this time the painter
focuses on the outlying industrial
area south of the city, on the other
side of the tracks that lead to the
Atocha railway station. This is
one of the districts that has
changed most drastically during
the twenty years Antonio López
worked on the composition,
actually transforming at the same
pace as the artist's pictorial motif,
a perfect example of how López'
oeuvre clings to reality as a
phenomenon determined by time.
Moreover, this is quite likely
one of the cityscapes in which
pictorial matter seems to
physically configure its motif,
freezing the view perceived by
the gaze as an accretion of time.

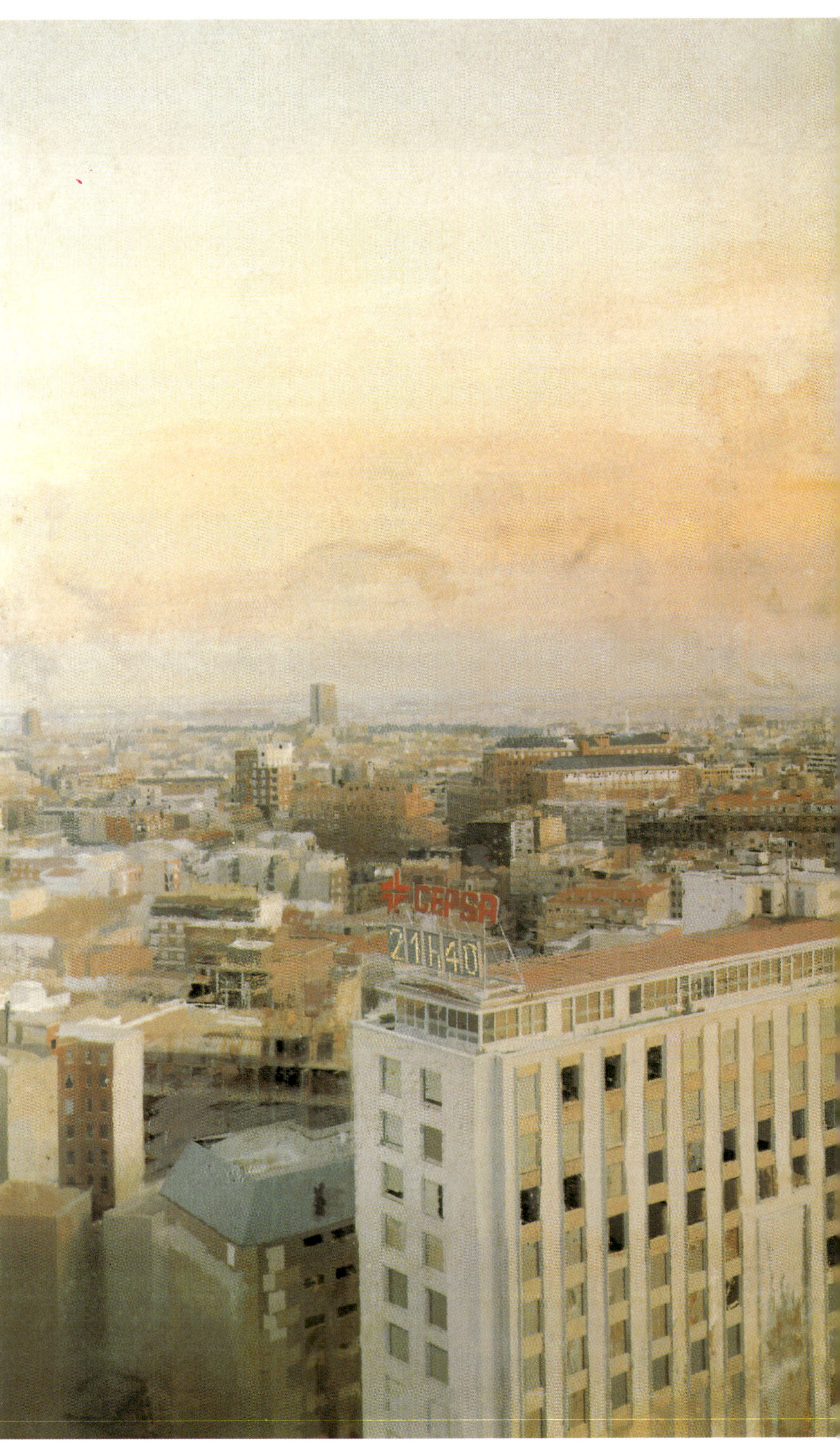

31. Madrid Seen from Torres Blancas, *1976–1982. This panorama depicts much of Madrid's expansion to the north seen from Torres Blancas, a skyscraper designed by the architect Sáenz de Oíza which was completed in the early seventies. Here we have no empty foreground, although we can still make out a few less well-defined areas, above all to the left of the composition. López' conception of painting and reality excludes the idea of the finished work — his pictures firmly depend on the artist's contemplation of his motif, which is usually (above all in the case of the city) dynamic and vibrant. The picture is completed when the artist decides to abandon it, aware as he is he can resume work on it, as time and the marks it leaves on things always have the upper hand.*

31

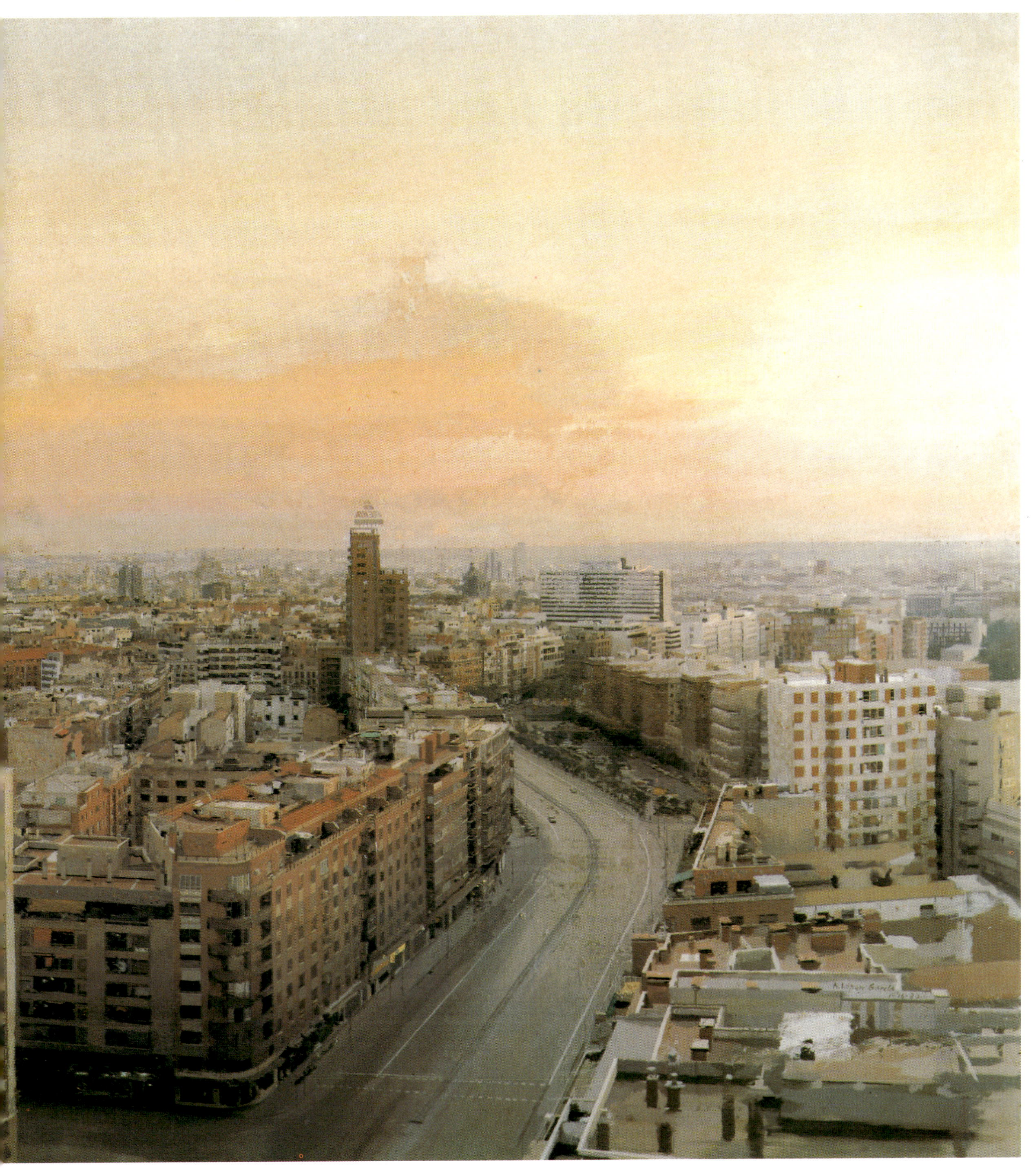

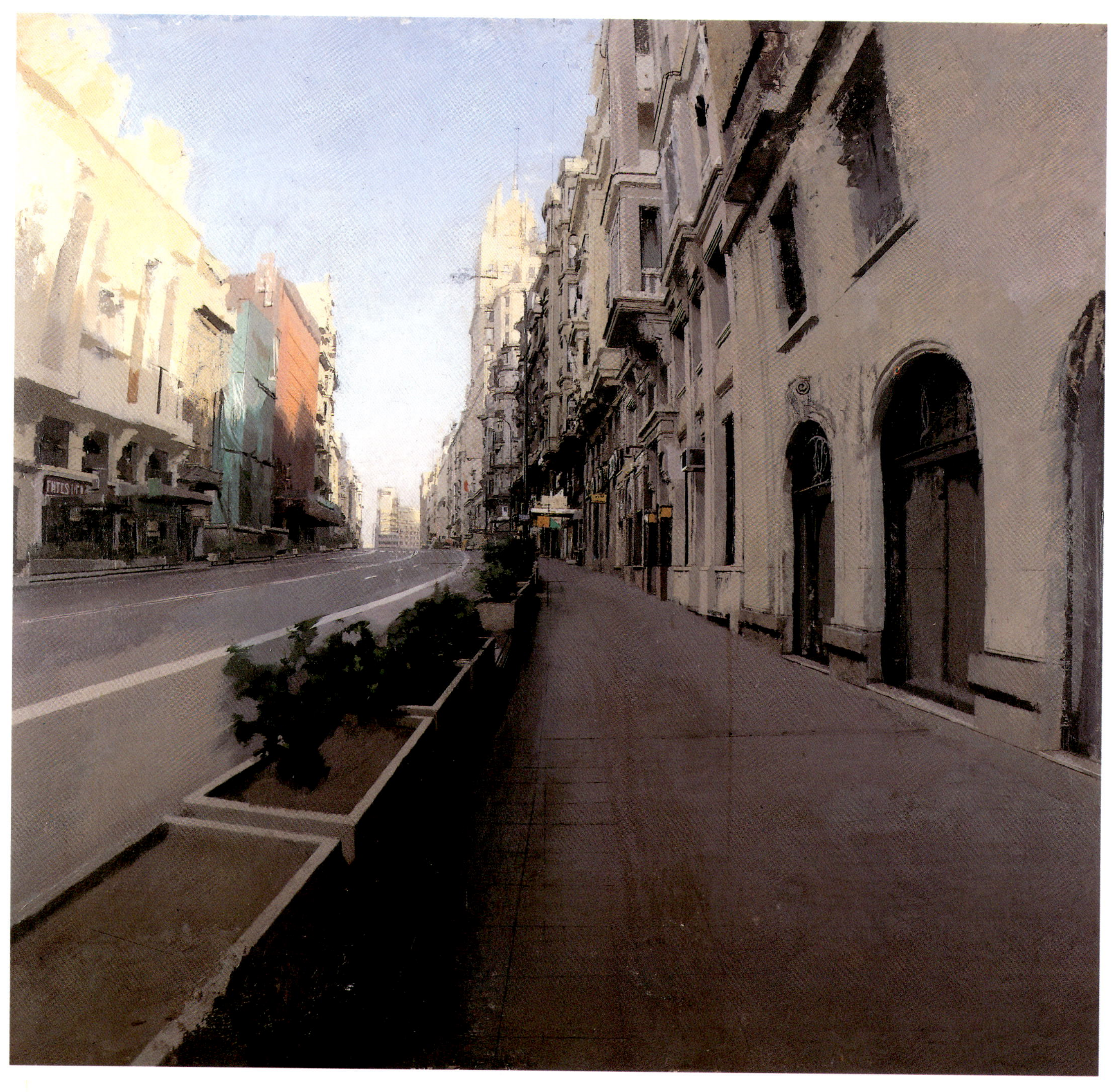

32

32–33. Gran Vía, Clavel, *1977–1990*. Gran Vía, *1974–1981*. *Two of the most well known cityscapes to have inspired Antonio López, painted in the first light of dawn. The second view depicts the beginning of the Gran Vía, one of the main arteries in the city centre. The same avenue appears in the first picture, captured towards the west, where it meets* calle Clavel. *In this work the rising sun thins down the upper area of the façades on the left, while the areas in shade are very well defined. The digital clock on Gran Vía (reading half-past six), also appears in* Madrid Seen from Torres Blancas, *adding a deliberate reference to time that affords the composition disturbing overtones.*

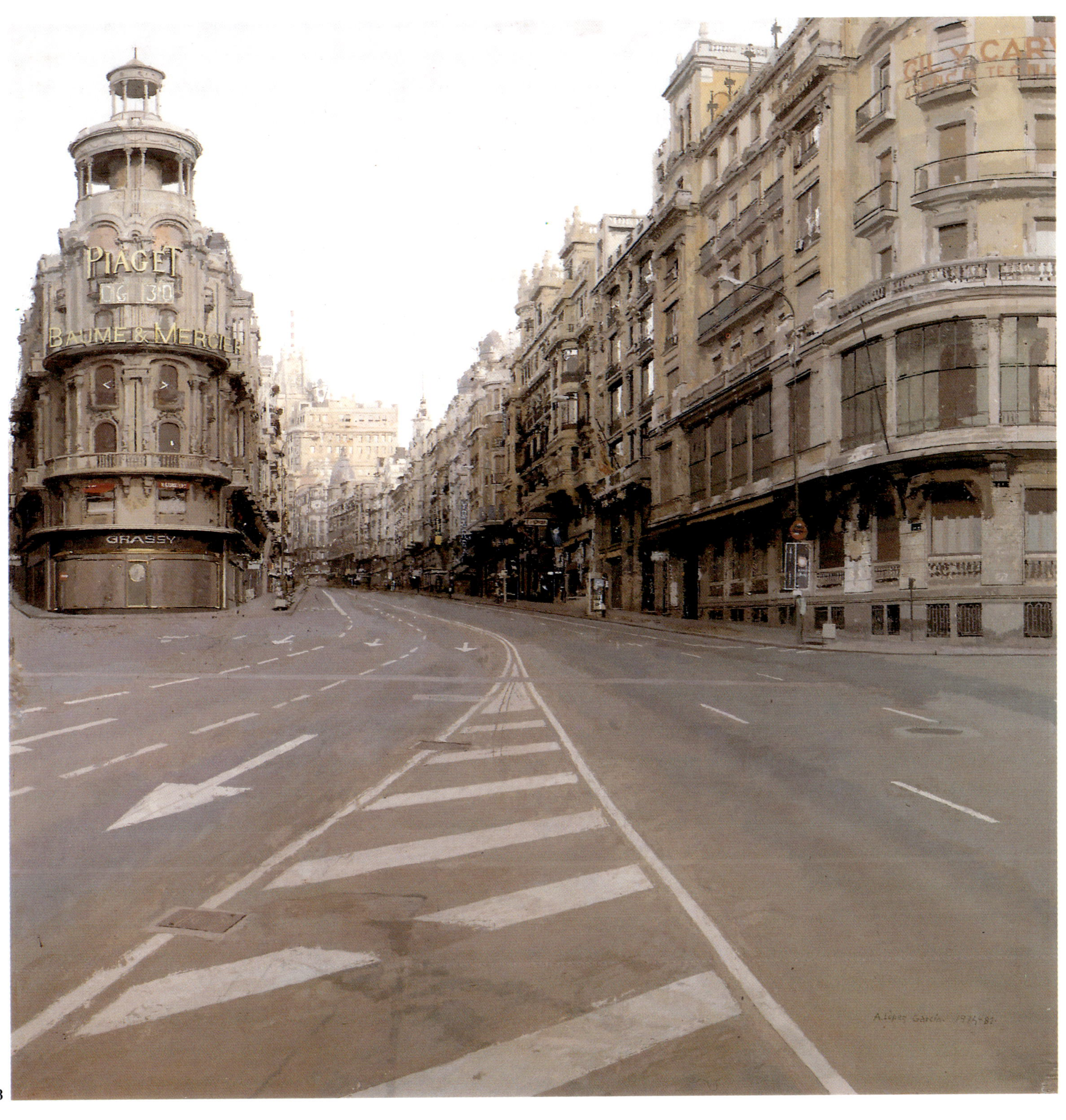

34. Campo del Moro, *1990. Thirty years before painting this scene Antonio López had already produced a view of this park, that looks on to the west façade of the Royal Palace. Still contaminated with a certain number of fantastic elements, his first version included two female figures floating in the sky, which have disappeared from this more recent rendering. The minute detail of the earlier work (despite the unreal mist enveloping the gardens) forms a sharp contrast with the clearer more synthetic approach of this composition, characterised by large areas of paint describing the green expanse.*

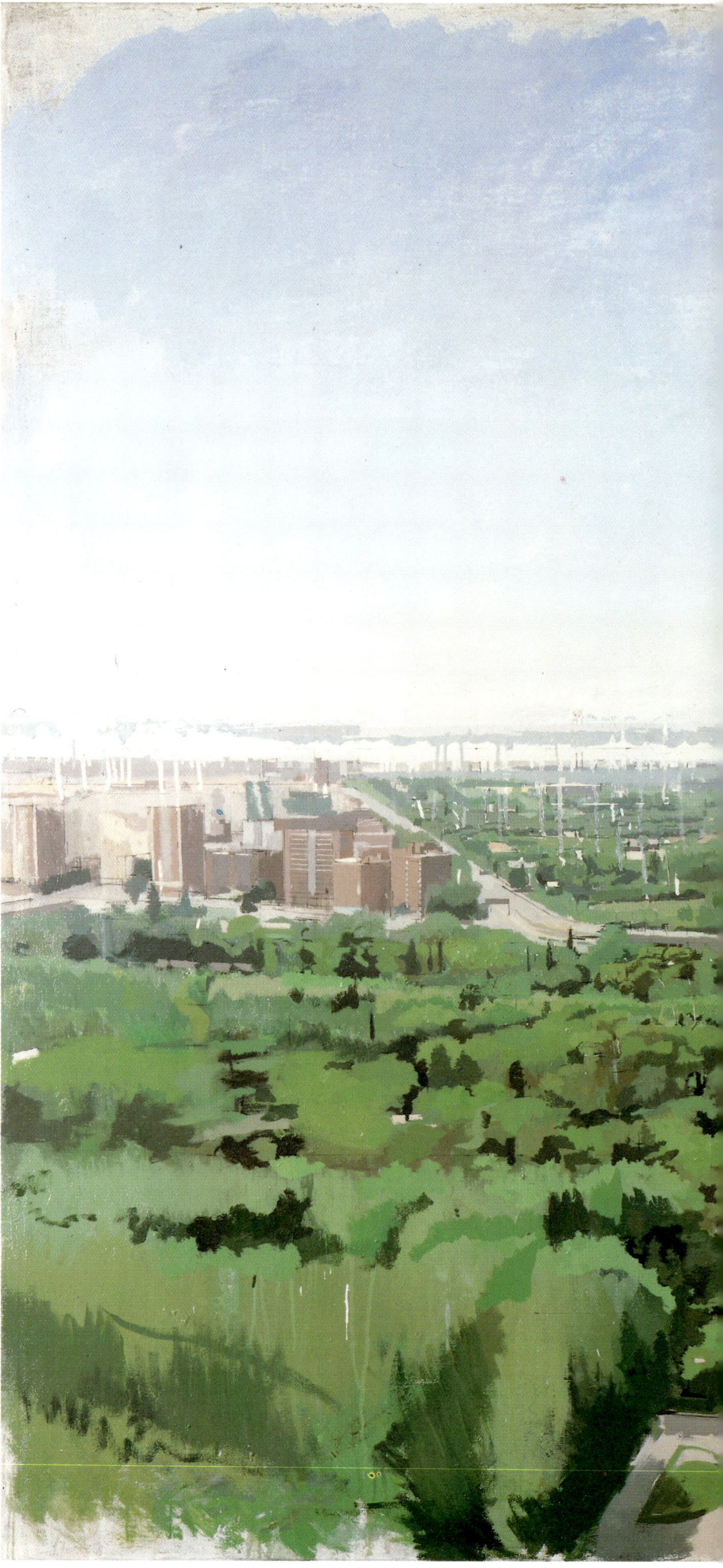

34

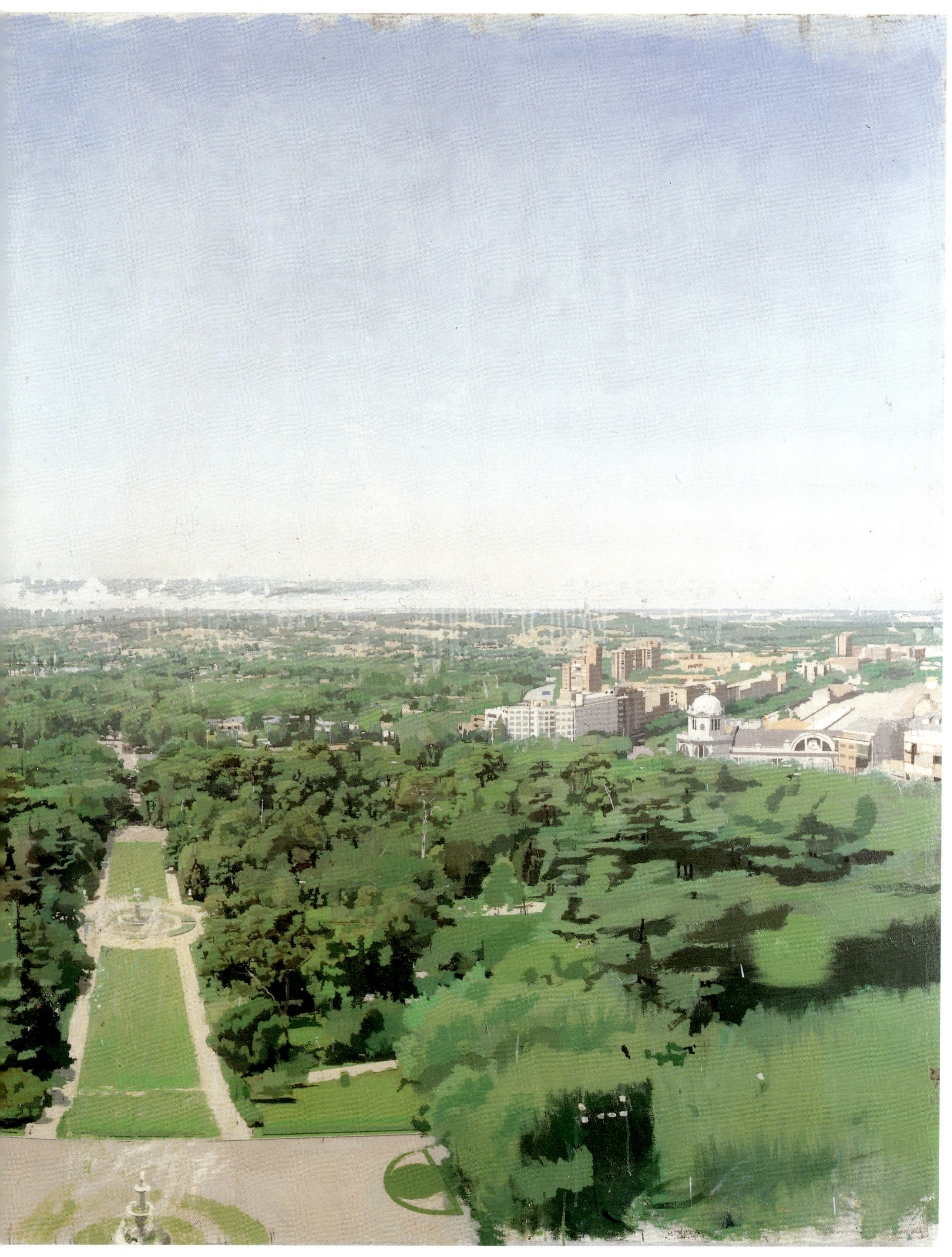

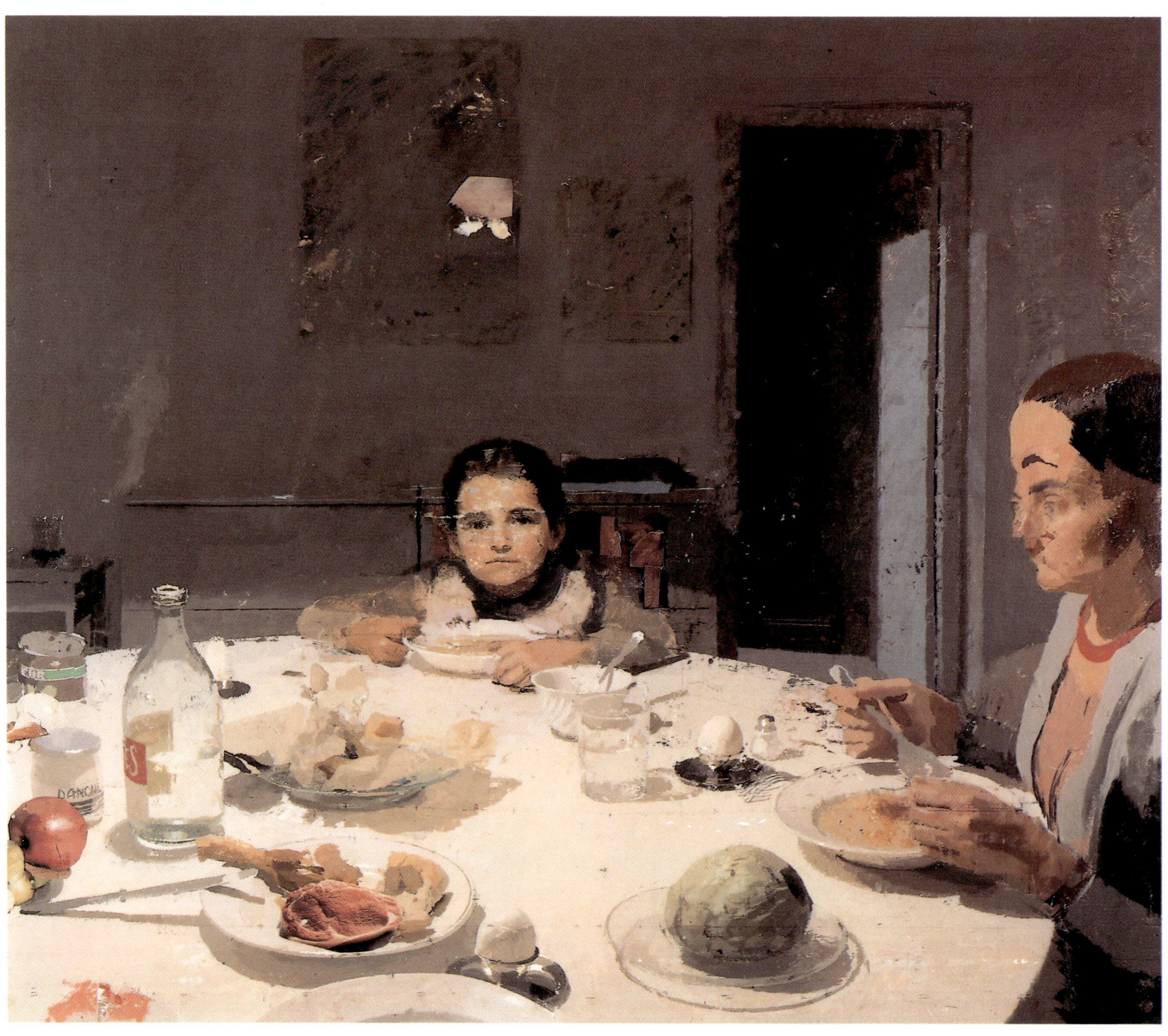

35

Intimate Spaces

Antonio López has confessed on more than one occasion that he tackles those themes that he considers particularly interesting or moving. Nonetheless, his choice of motifs is also determined by the demands made by his conception of painting: objects, views and spaces susceptible of remaining stationary before the artist's eyes while he paints them. This explains his preference for places and events taken from his domestic environment — his family, his studio, his friends' houses — and the reappearance of the complex relations between his painting and time, exemplified by the growing-up of his daughters, the consequences of the passing of time on the walls of the terrace roof of his friend Lucio Muñoz, and the traces of activity in his empty studio. His painting condenses time in a motionless present that suddenly reveals the enigmatic, conflicting and non-apprehensible nature of reality. As postwar American Abstract painters began to do, Antonio López usually prefers large-scale formats, that eventually turn out to be man's true scale, where representation comes disturbingly close to ordinary perception.

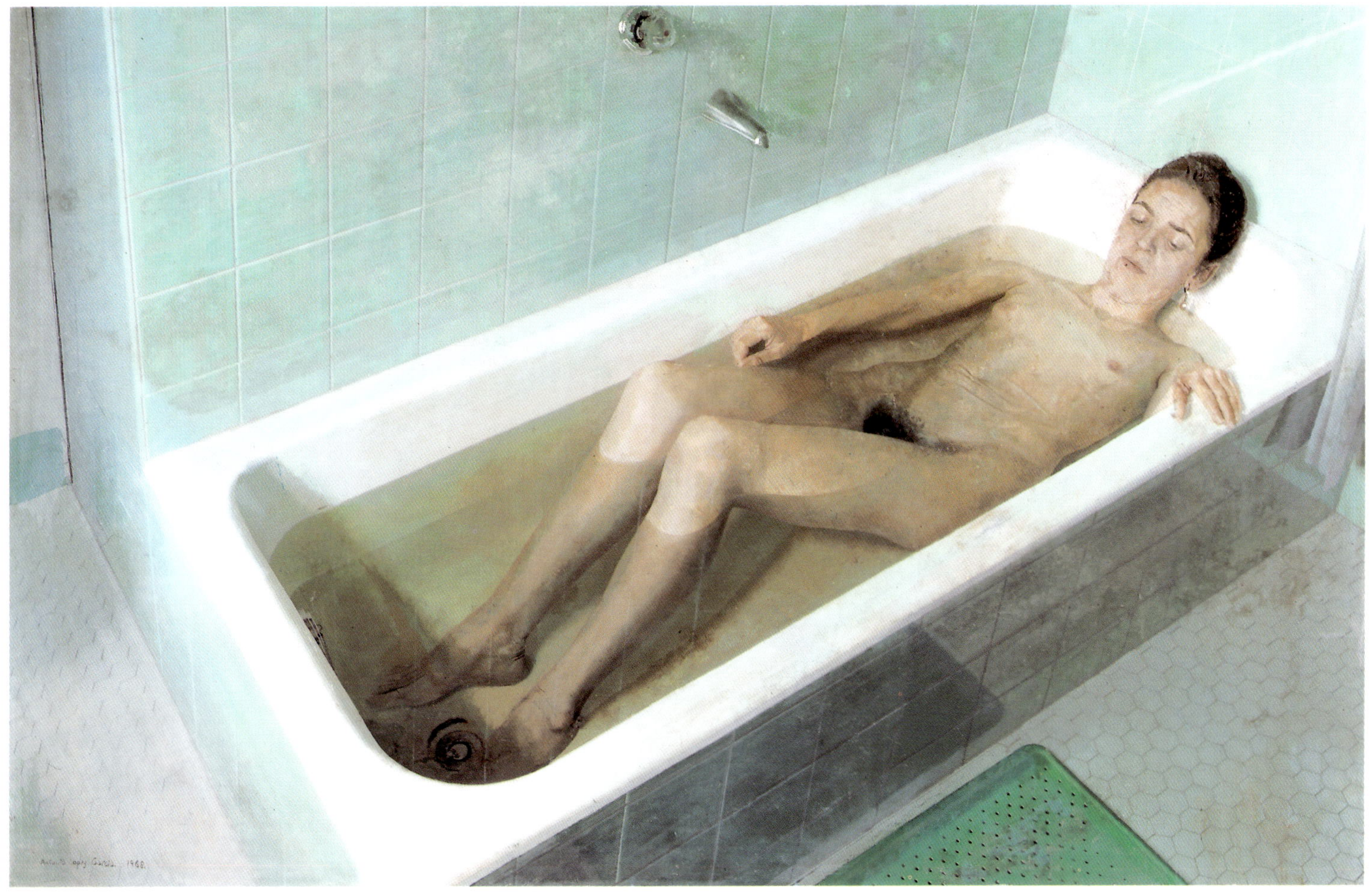

35. Supper, *1971–1980. This scene of an evening meal is depicted from the point of view of one of the members of the family. While the paint seems to merge into the consistency and texture of each of the foodstuffs, the pictorial process is thrown into relief by the two superimposed positions of the head of the figure on the right. The end result, of this and of other works, is an accumulation of successive pictorial sessions.*

36. Woman in the Bath, *1968. This is another bathroom scene, dominated by the effects of electric light in a tiled interior. The whole composition is a play on smooth and imprecise textures — the ripples of water on the naked body, the reflection of the bath mat and the curtains on the tiles. As in* Hand Basin *and in* Clothes in Soak, *the painter employs forced close-up angles that enhance the intensity of the image.*

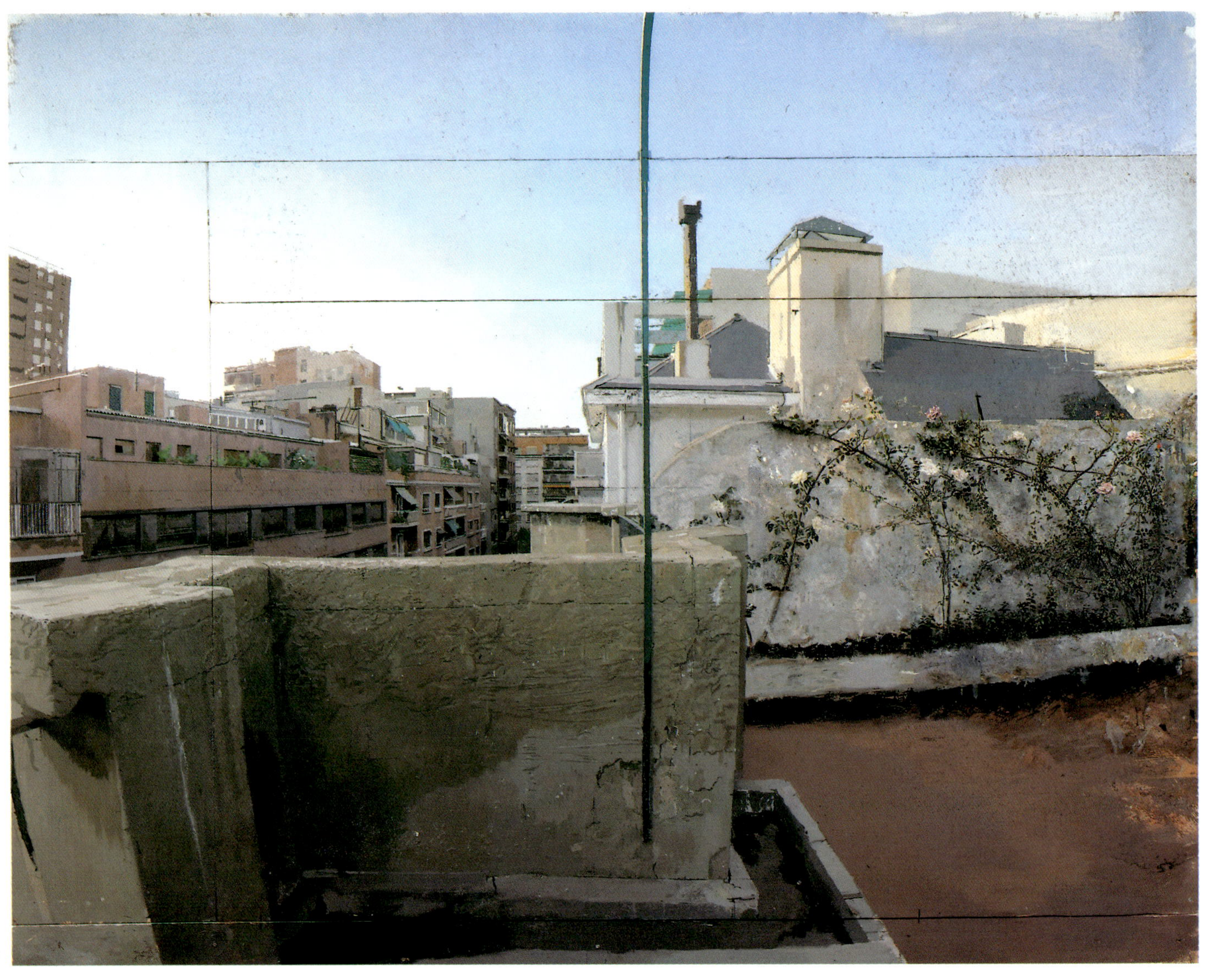

37. Lucio's Roof Terrace, *1962–1990. Antonio López began this picture in 1962, intending it to be a setting in which to portray his friends Lucio Muñoz and Amalia Avia, together with their son and Eusebio Sempere, who were "very close friends, very young people at a happy time of their lives. I began by painting the walls, the ground, the roof-garden full of flowers." Years later he returned to the flat, where his friends no longer lived. "It had all changed greatly, not the various features, which remained the same, but their appearance and perhaps even my way of looking (…). I have had to alter most of the picture, adding new areas above, below and to the left to ensure the convergence of the vanishing lines. The main feature of the work was now the effect of time on the walls, the crack letting in the dark street, the granulated cement of the terrace wall on the left, that seems to surge forward to the point of enabling the viewer to reach out and touch it."*

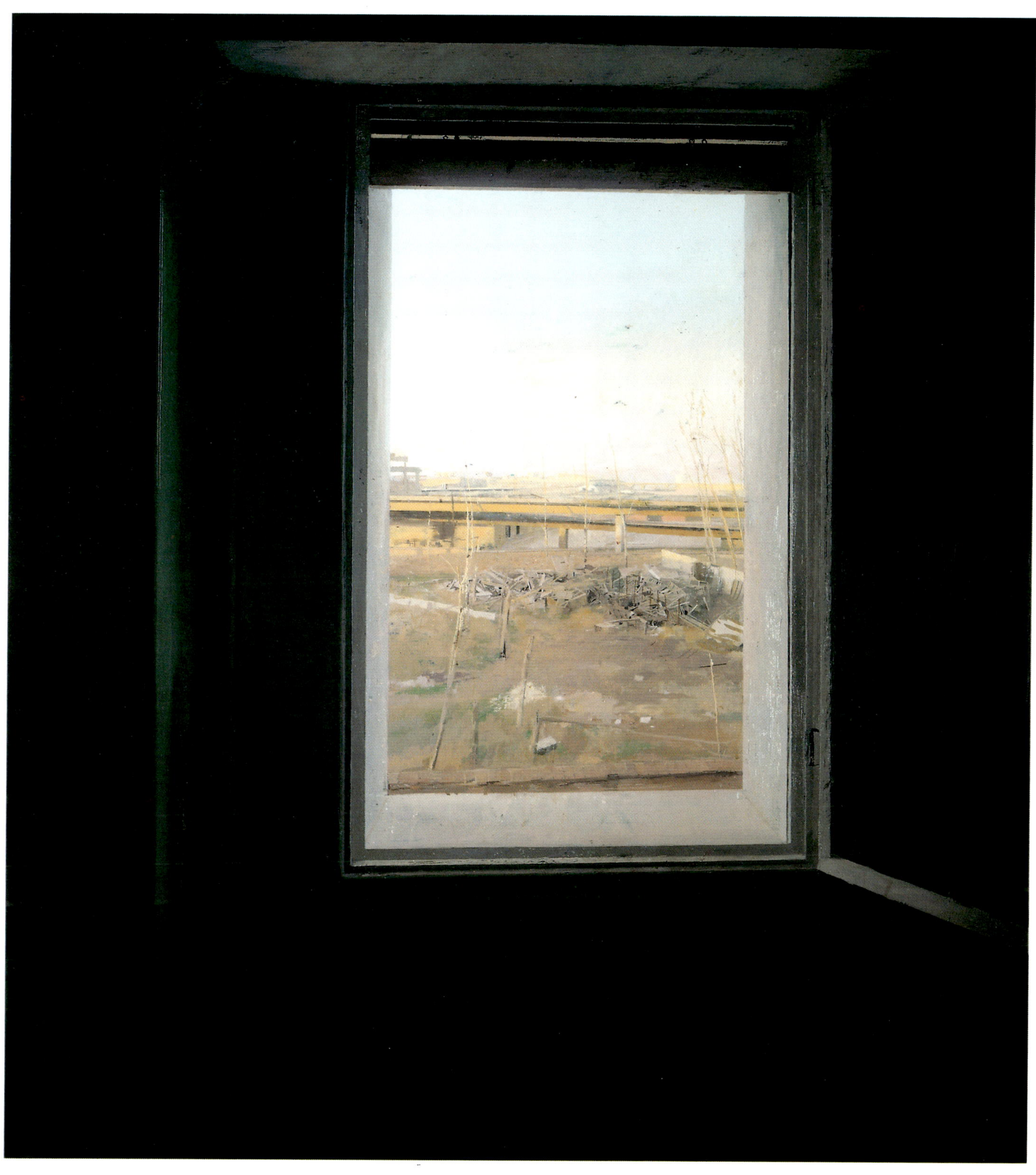

38. Afternoon Window, *1974–1982. In the eighties our artist dedicated several
works to the window as a motif, one of the traditional metaphors in painting since
the treatise drawn up by Leon Battista Alberti in the fifteenth century. In the case
of Antonio López, the windows are always those of his studio, through which he
observes a peripheral city landscape. Once again, the main theme is the passage
of time, the contrast between interior and exterior lighting, and the painter's
innermost reflections on painting as an instrument by means of which to
represent an elusive ever-changing reality.*

39. Studio with Three Doors, *1969–1970. Once again we
are before a domestic interior, this time drawn in pencil.
The symmetry of the three doors, one of them closed,
introduces a disturbing element that forms a sharp
contrast with the ordinary nature of the setting. In spite
of the presence of two shades of colour, the fidelity with
which the space has been clearly defined by means of
light is quite extraordinary.*

40. Vase with Flowers and Wall, *1965. As he would do later
in some of his bathroom scenes, on this occasion the artist
juxtaposes two different images with independent spatial
rules that do, however, tend to be interpreted jointly,
thereby creating an obvious ambiguity.*

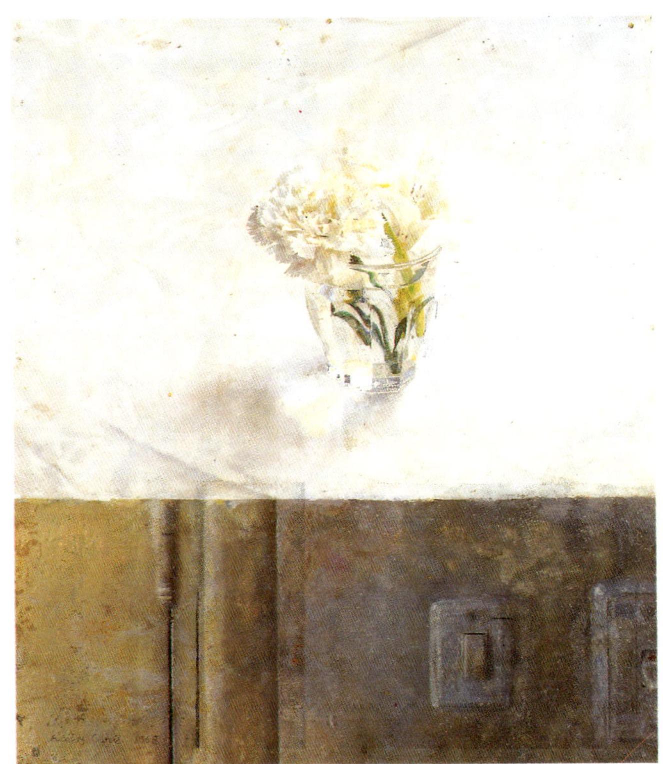

40

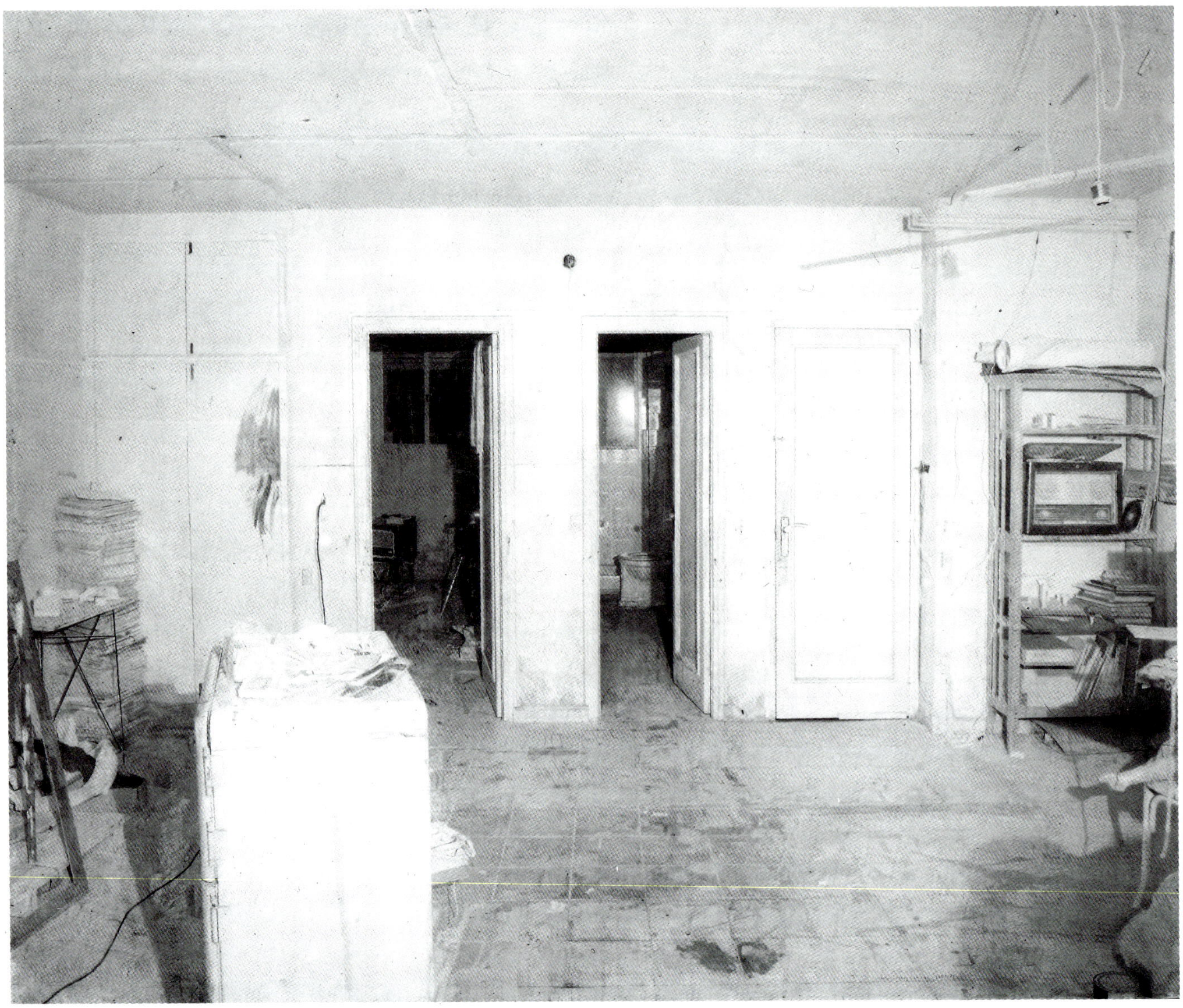

39

41

41. Electric Light, *1970. This is a complementary image to* Studio with Three Doors, *in which the studio is now seen from the area within one of the doors depicted in the previous drawing. The lit room, a true display of the artist's virtuosity in portraying reflections and shadows upon tiled surfaces, sets up an enigmatic dialogue with the pinpoint of the light bulb struggling for visibility amidst the semidarkness of the background.*

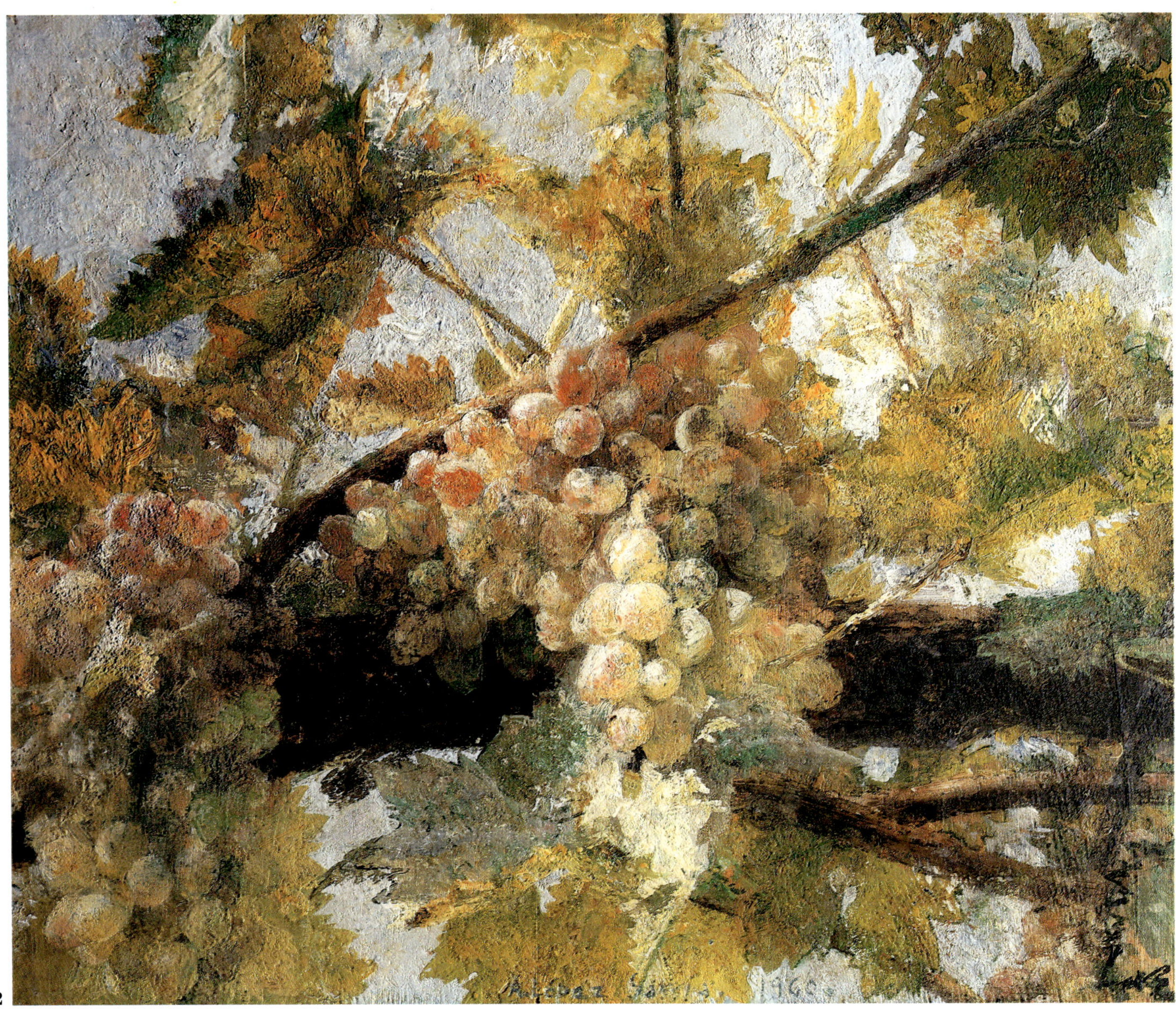

42

The Garden

One of the endless sources of pictorial motifs for Antonio López is his garden. From the very beginning of his career he had revealed his taste for a close observation of flowers, plants and fruit trees, producing works of an intensity unprecedented in the painters who had hitherto frequented the genre. Such motifs, that constitute one of the less familiar areas of the artist's work, afford him the opportunity of experimenting the encounter with physical reality on another scale, observing the effect of the most delicate nuances of light on rose petals or the growth of a quince. Plants are living organisms and their life cycles are indissolubly related to the seasons, so we have another example of the ongoing relationship between painting and time. This is what led Víctor Erice to make the feature film *El sol del membrillo* in 1992, where he captures the painter's fight against time as he strives to paint a quince tree, one of his favourite plant motifs, a struggle that invariably ends in a fertile defeat. Although these pictures have the appearance of studies, the artist does not approach them as means to an end but as totally independent works.

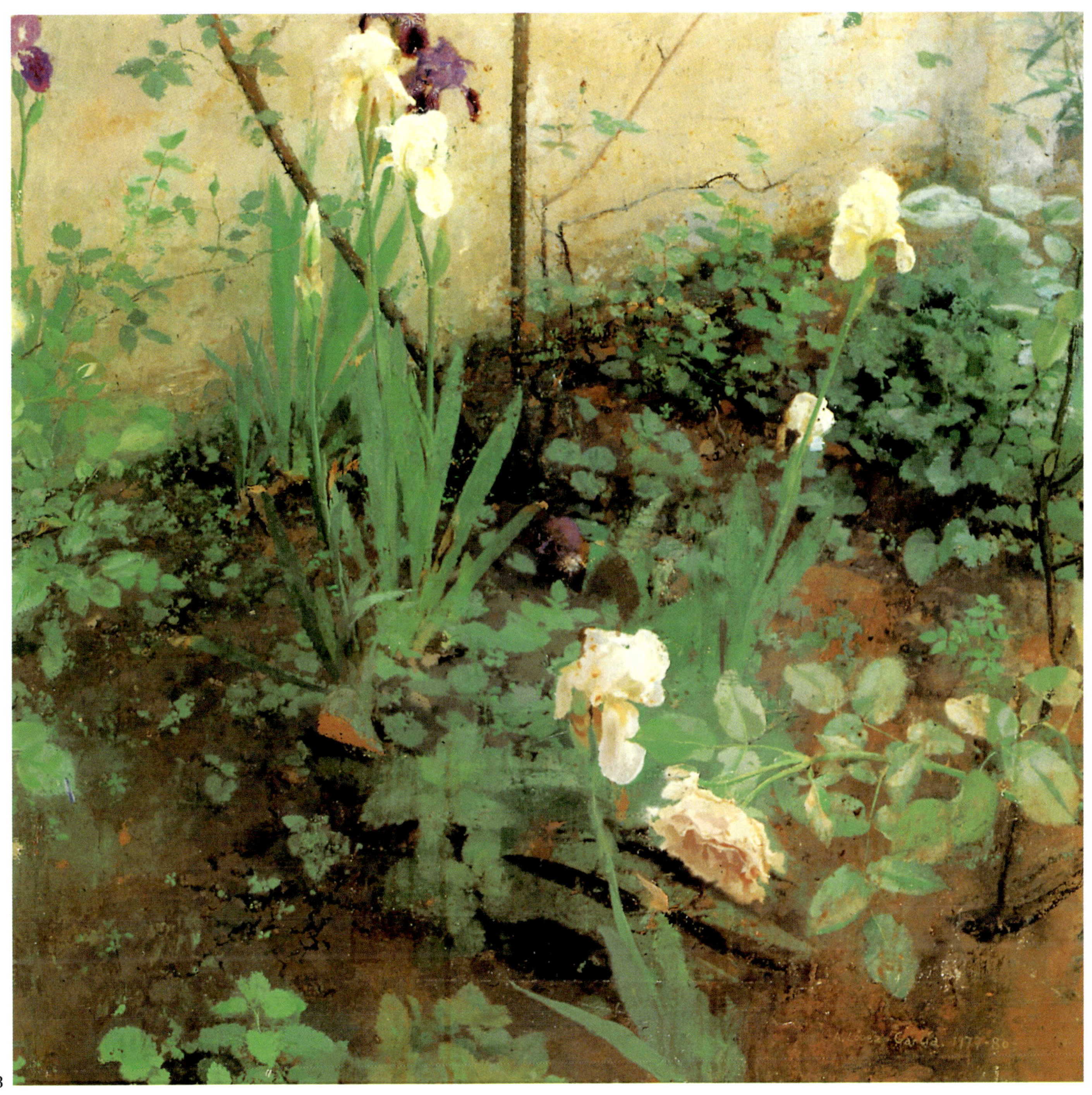

43

42. The Vine, *1955. This is one of the earliest examples of the artist's taste
for depicting plants and fruit from very close range. Vines are particularly
characteristic of La Mancha wine region, the painter's homeland. In almost
Cézannesque fashion, López structures this picture by means of uneven planes
of colour, the interaction of which transforms the values of form and volume
into a perfectly balanced plastic configuration.*

43. Irises and Roses, *1977–1980. In spite of the extreme concentration of the
artist's gaze, this picture accurately conveys the idea of a corner space halfway
between light and shade. The graceful capturing of the light flickering on the
petals and the sense of immediacy are actually the result of an intense process
of observation and elaboration, as proven by the three years elapsed between the
beginning and completion of the work.*

44. Rear Garden, 1969. Impressive in its starkness, the garden at the close of winter is an image that entails the promise of the flowers and leaves that will soon begin to grow again, as we see in the timid shoots emerging on some of the branches. Few pictures devoted to this subject matter present such a convincing description of the cyclical changing of the seasons, an almost cosmogonical idea that has interested painters of all ages, approached here by López in his characteristically sober manner.

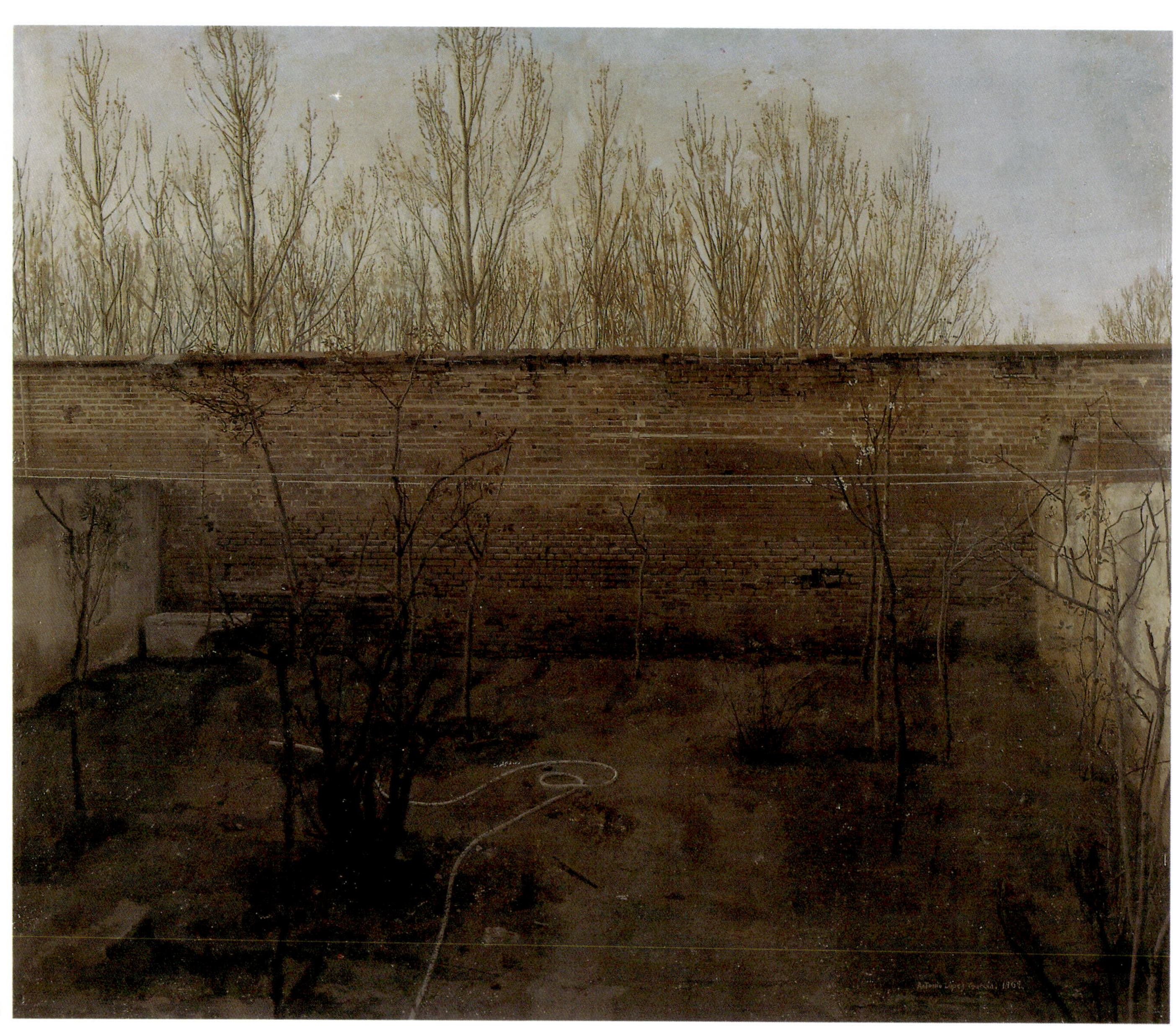

44

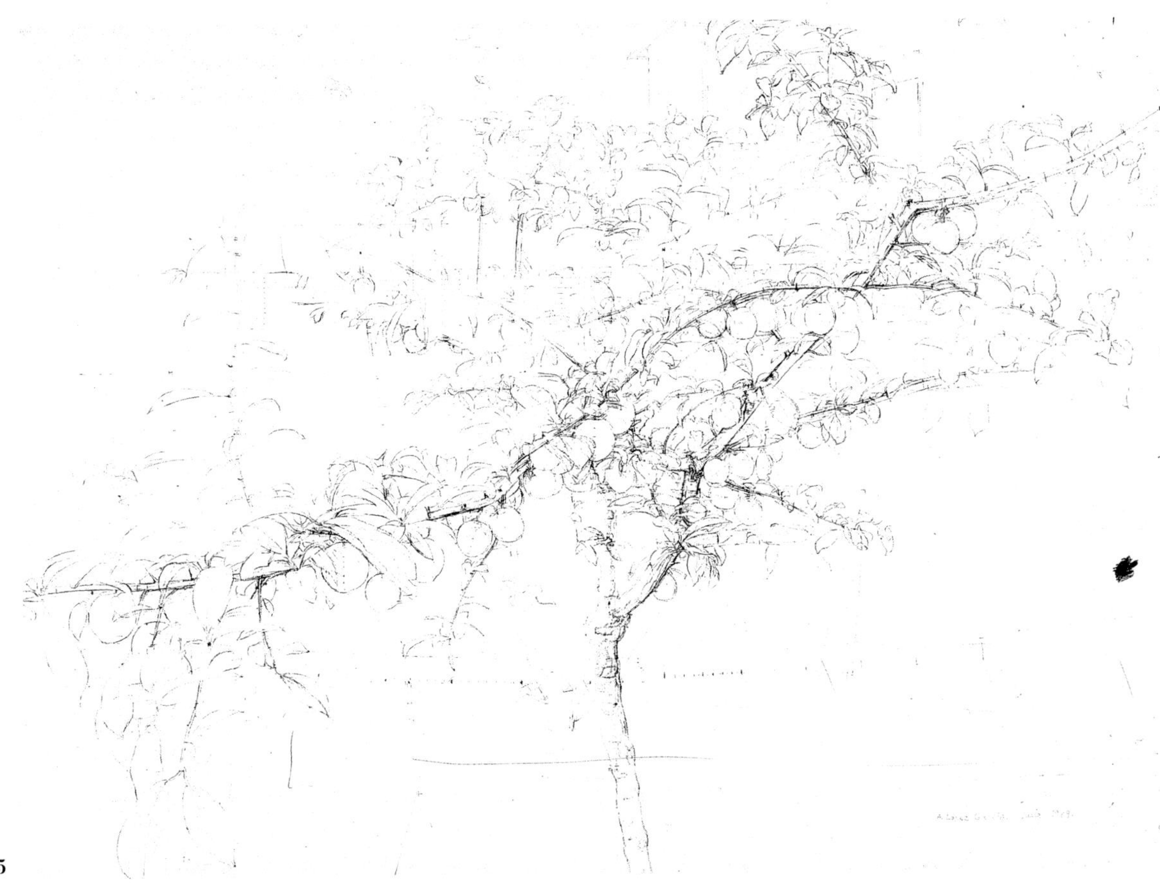

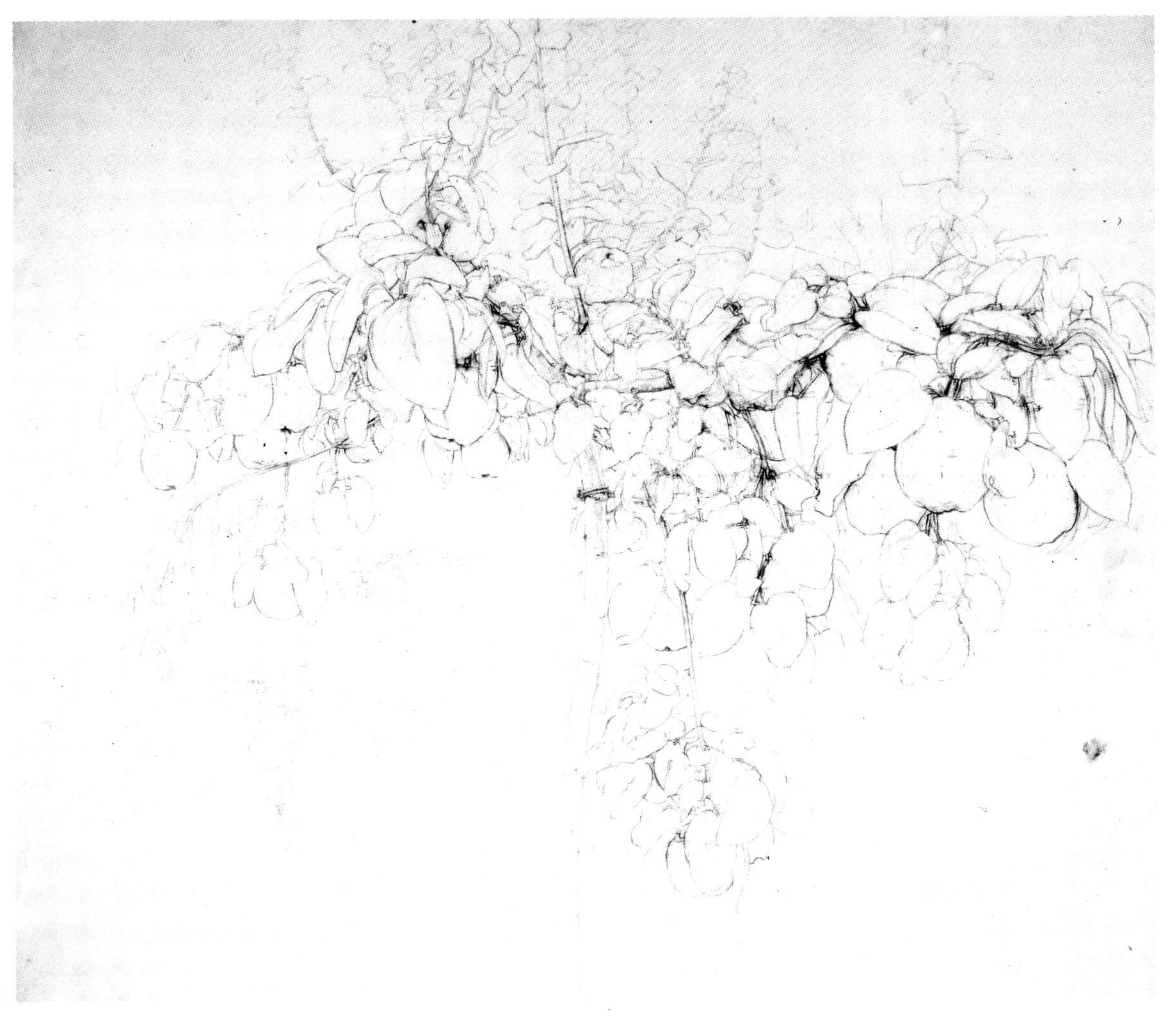

45–46. Plum Tree, *1989.*
Quince Tree, *1990. In these
two drawings Antonio
López has dispensed with
all effects of shading and
modelling, exploring
instead a calligraphic
language that brings to
mind Japanese works in
the genre. With extreme
delicacy, López thickens
and condenses line in
order to render the volume
and layout of branches,
leaves and fruit in space.*

Antonio López. Sculptor

"I don't consider myself a true painter, a pure painter," the artist told Michael Brenson. "More than colour, the shape of things, their volume, matter and the distance between their different areas have always been the stimuli prompting my pictures, and all this is probably what has enabled me to work as a sculptor." Antonio López began to model in the round and in relief from the very beginning of his career. The physical reality of sculpture, as opposed to the mediating fiction of painting, provided the Castilian artist with a new ground for his encounter with reality. Although his fascination with Egyptian and Ancient Greek statuary is obvious, reliefs (often painted) constitute an intermediate phase between the two disciplines, a phase which would prove amazingly productive. As in his paintings, López tackles his material directly, life-size, dispensing with sketches and preparatory studies. His motifs match those characterising his pictorial oeuvre, although the human figure does seem to prevail in works that seek a compromise between the presence of generic and specific traits.

47–48. The Apparition of the Younger Brother, 1959. The Apparition, 1963. The origin of both reliefs lies in a legend set in Tomelloso, according to which the parents of a dead child reported apparitions of their son. Antonio López learnt the story from his aunts and devoted a couple of works to the subject. The bronze version is somewhat restricted by the conventions of the support (critics have mentioned the influence of Ghiberti, Donatello and other Renaissance sculptors), while the polychromed wood sculpture is virtually a painted relief, characterised by the same material quality and nuances of the artist's two-dimensional compositions.

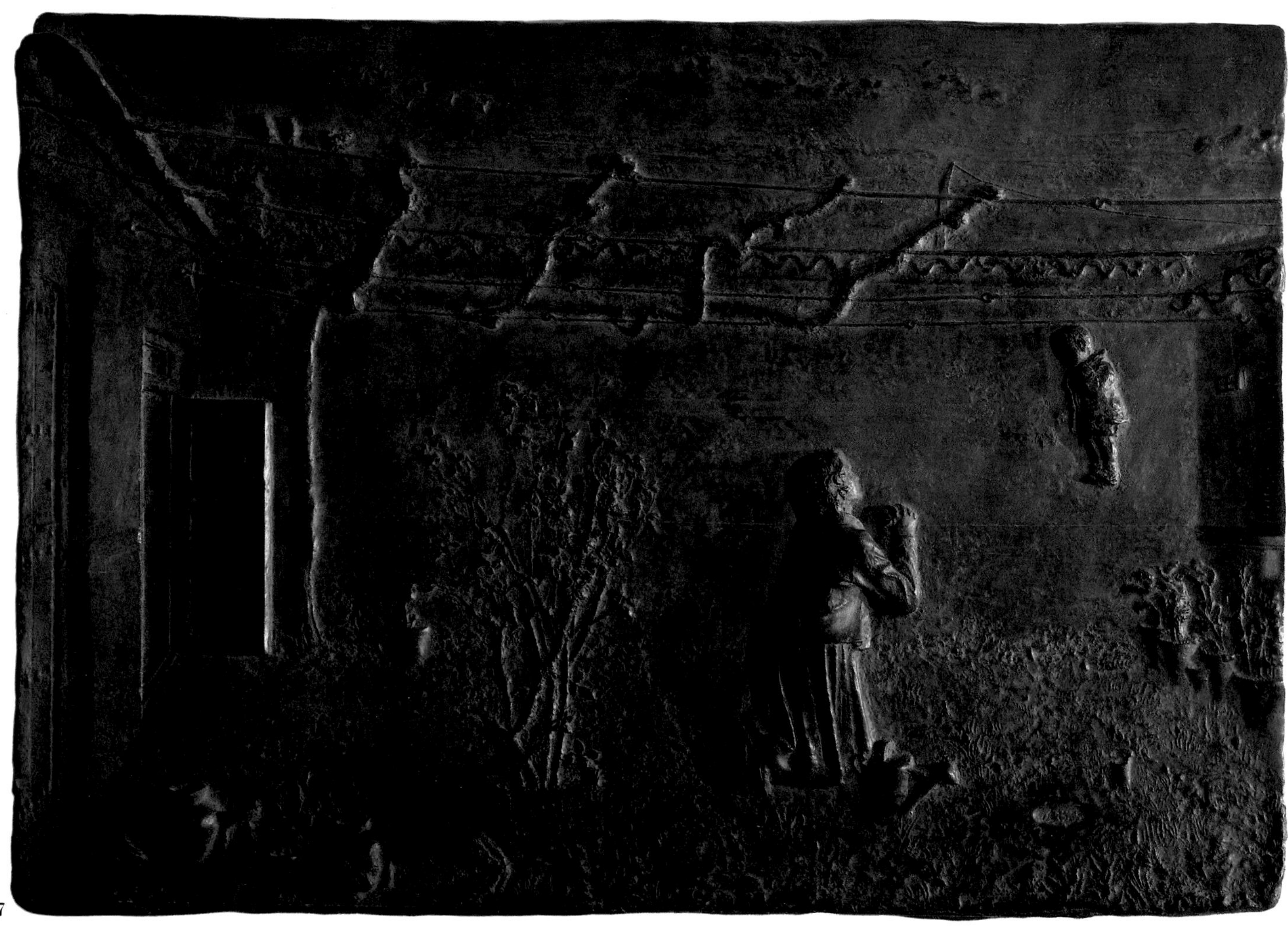

47

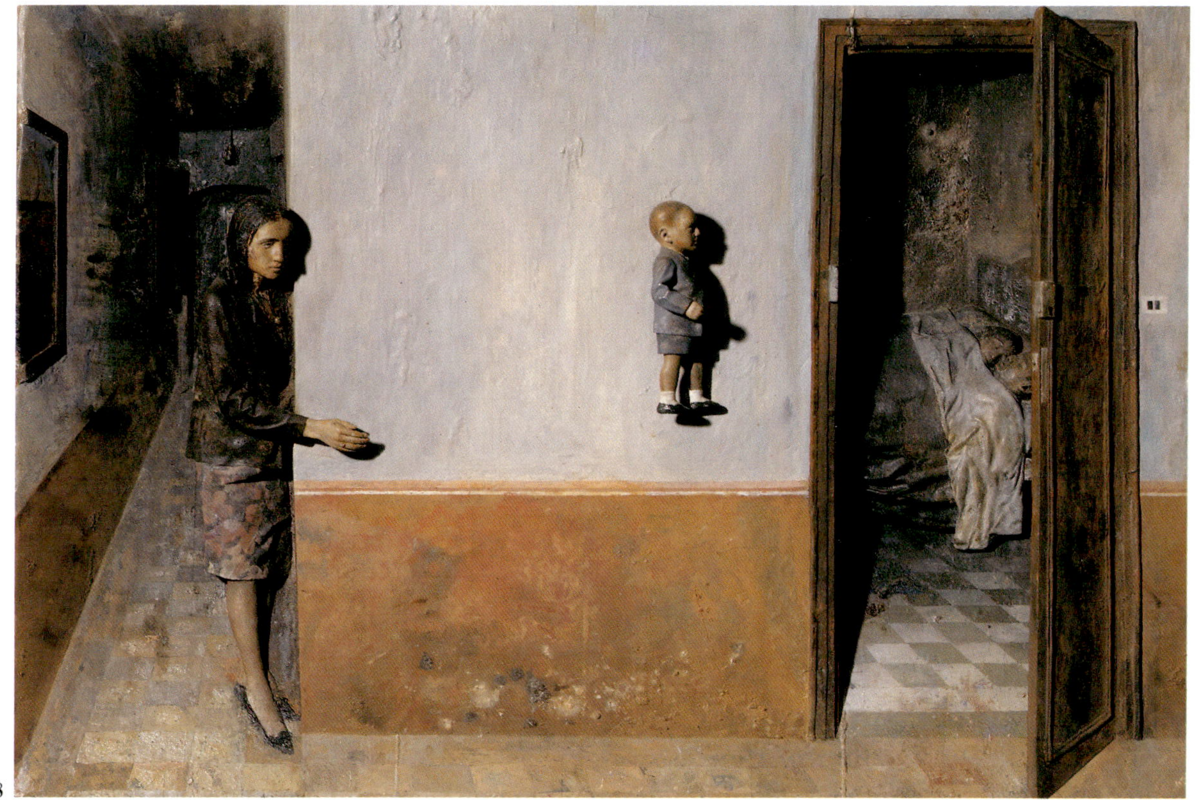

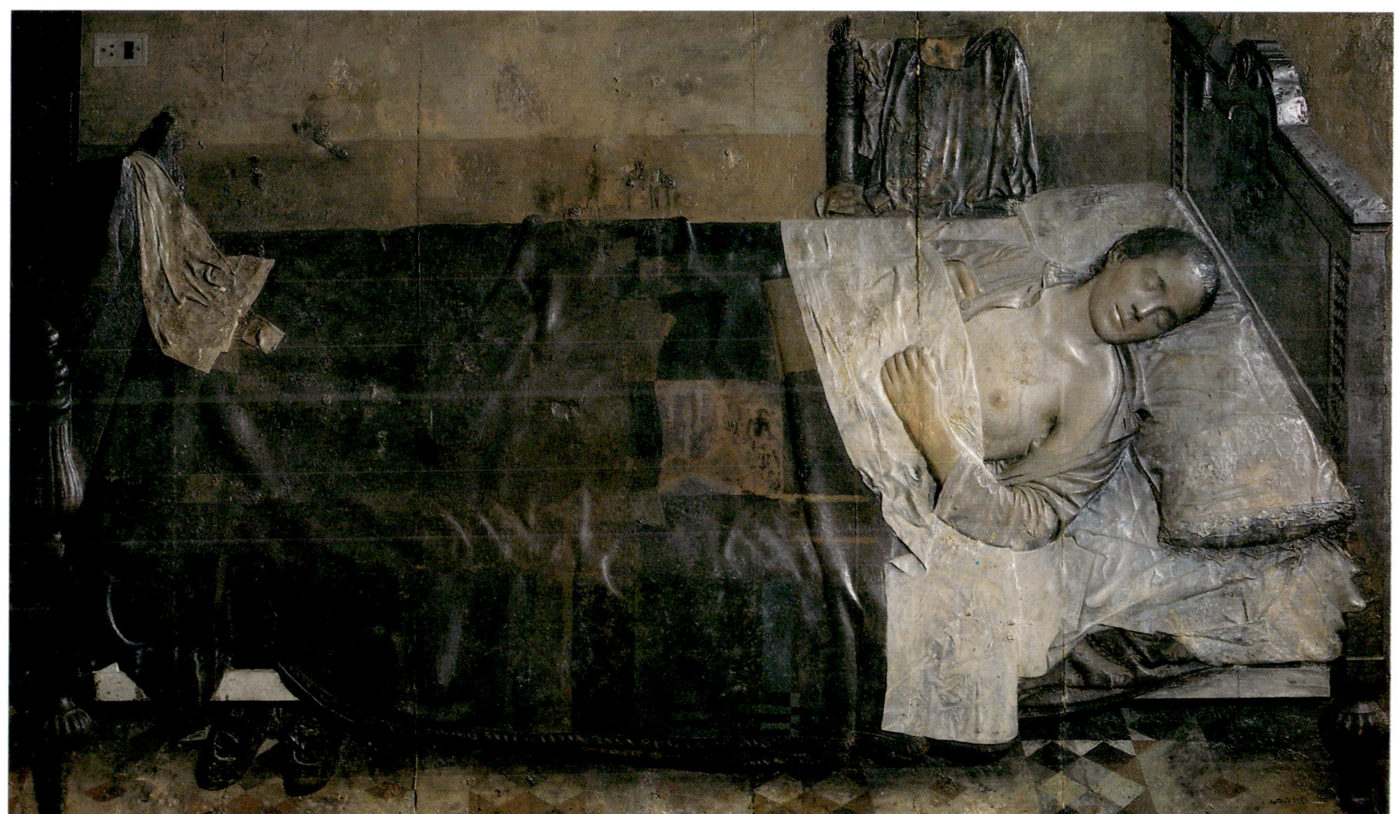

49. Sleeping Woman, *1963. Volume and texture in this sculpture of polychromed wood is less pictorialist than their counterparts in* The Apparition. *Once again the artist has executed a bronze version of the same motif, which presents only slight variations with respect to the wooden carving and the work cast in plaster.*

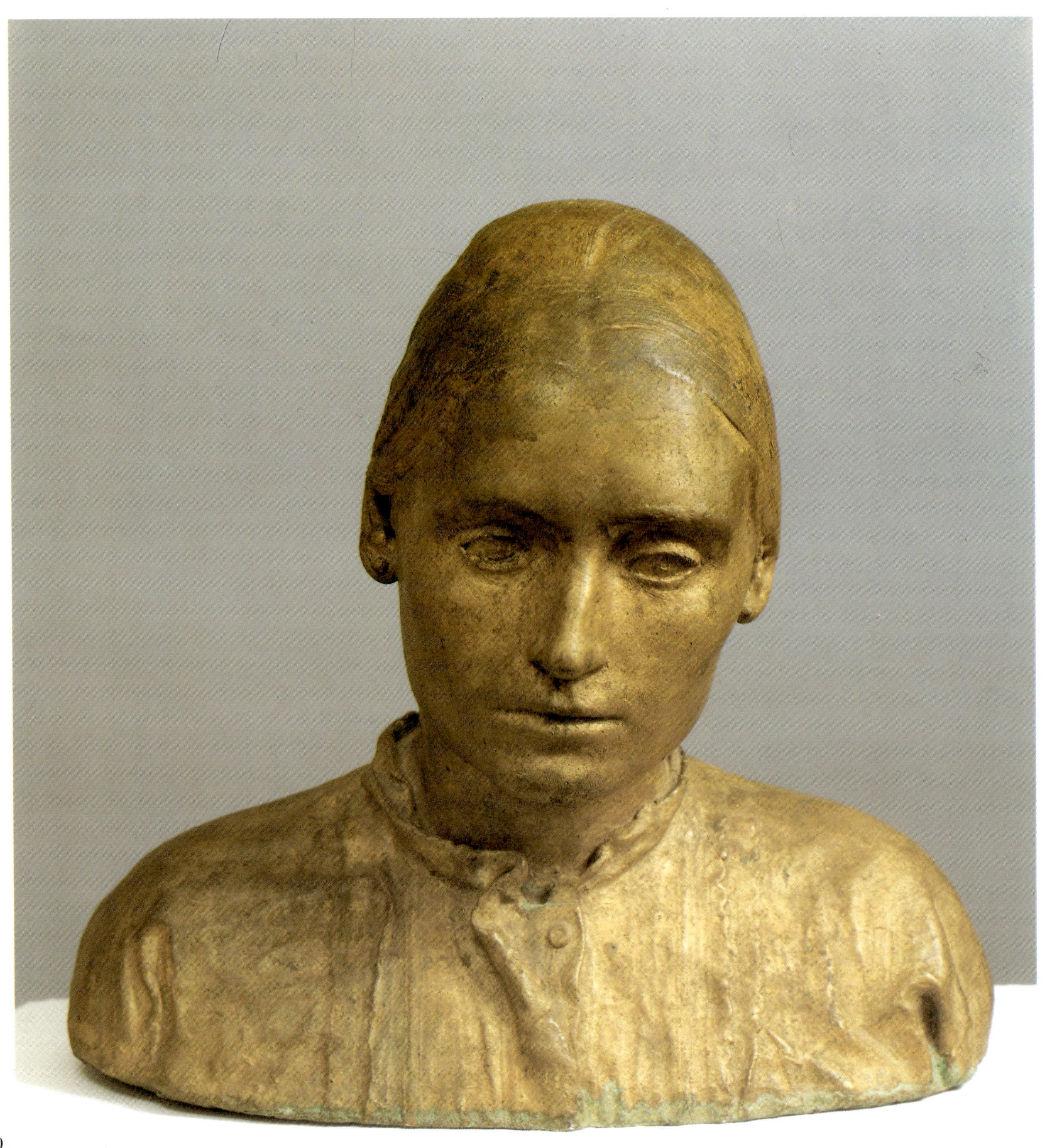

50

*50. Mari, 1961. This bronze bust of the artist's wife, María Moreno, is another
of the sculptures that bring to mind Italian Renaissance bronzes, in particular
thanks to López' categorical yet synthetic volumes. The serene neutral expression
of the face, however, has more in common with his taste for Egyptian sculpture
and its direct rendering of reality through a limited number of formal resources.*

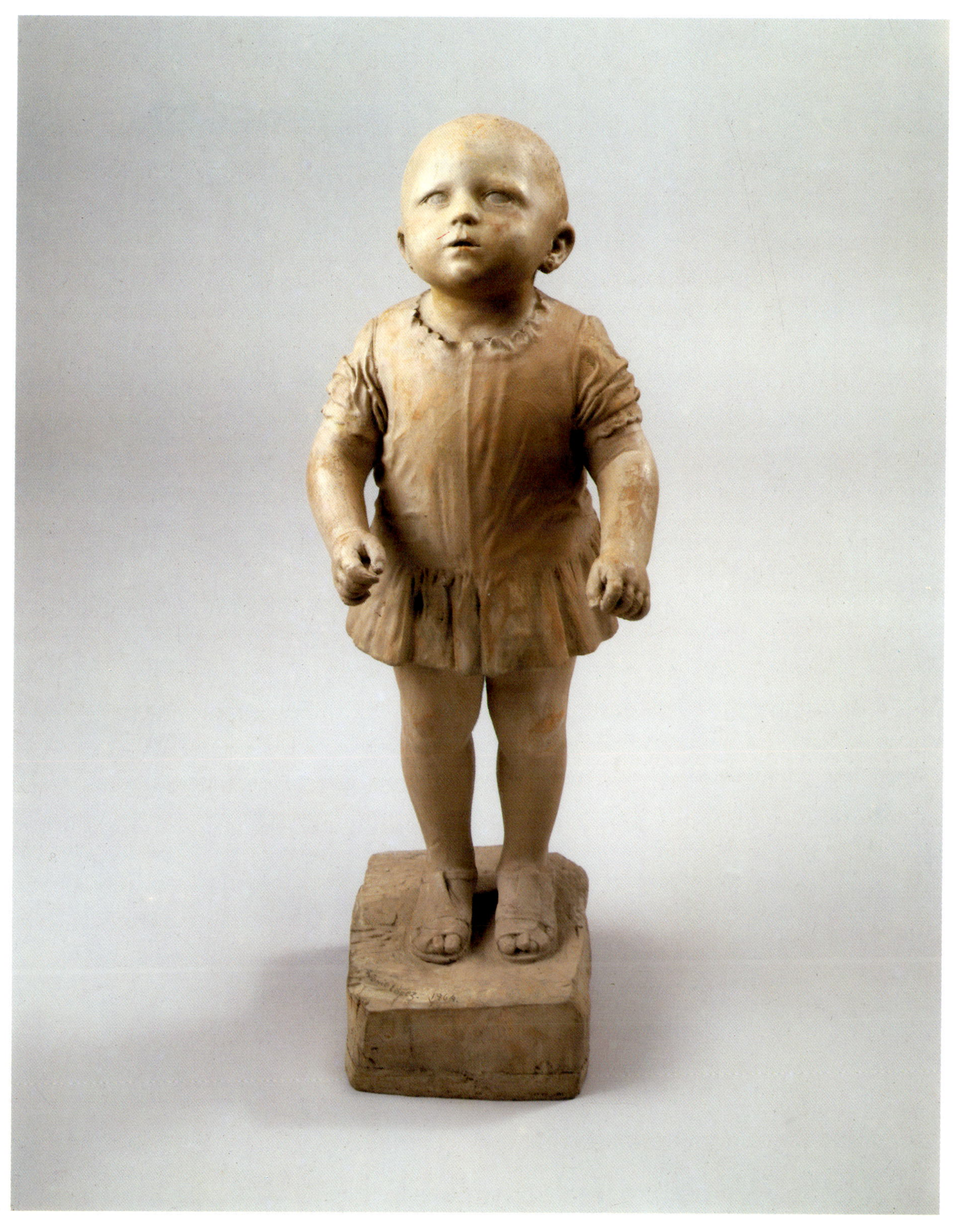

51. María Standing, 1963. In bronze as in wood, Antonio López pays utmost attention to the finish and patina of his works, attaining the same material effects afforded by his painted surfaces. The motif here is a life-size representation of his elder daughter when she was barely one year old. The discreetly classical face movingly captures the candid gesture of toddlers taking their first magical steps, who tend to raise their eyes in the hope of finding a reassuring adult presence.

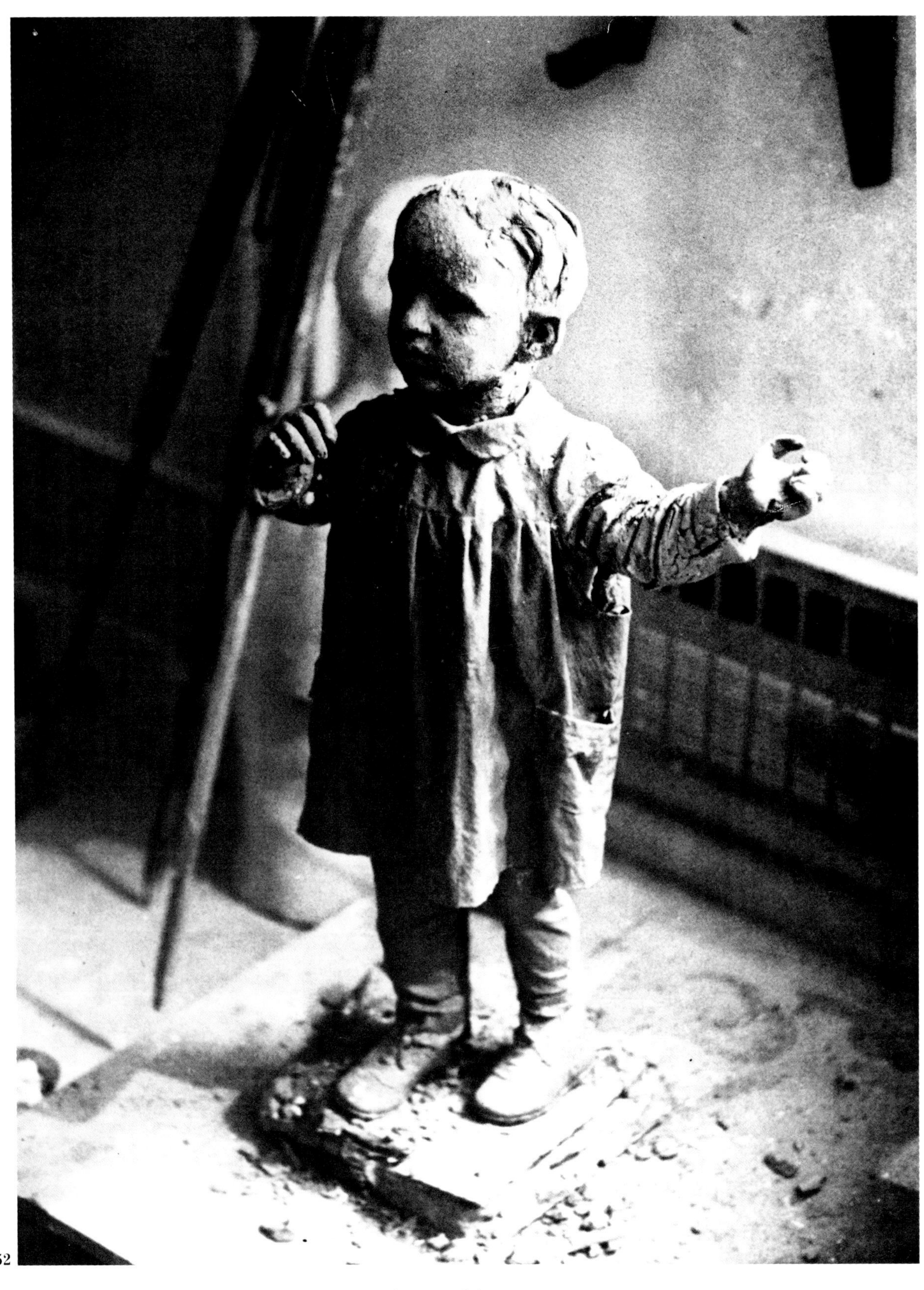

52. Carmencita, *1965–1968. This sculptural image of the artist's youngest daughter is another faithful and tender representation of the precarious balance children attain as they learn to take their first steps. The technical challenge is greater on this occasion, perhaps as a result of the outstretched left hand, that distinguishes this sculpture from the previous rather more inert figure, while the folds and pleats of the dress endow the statue with expressive light effects.*

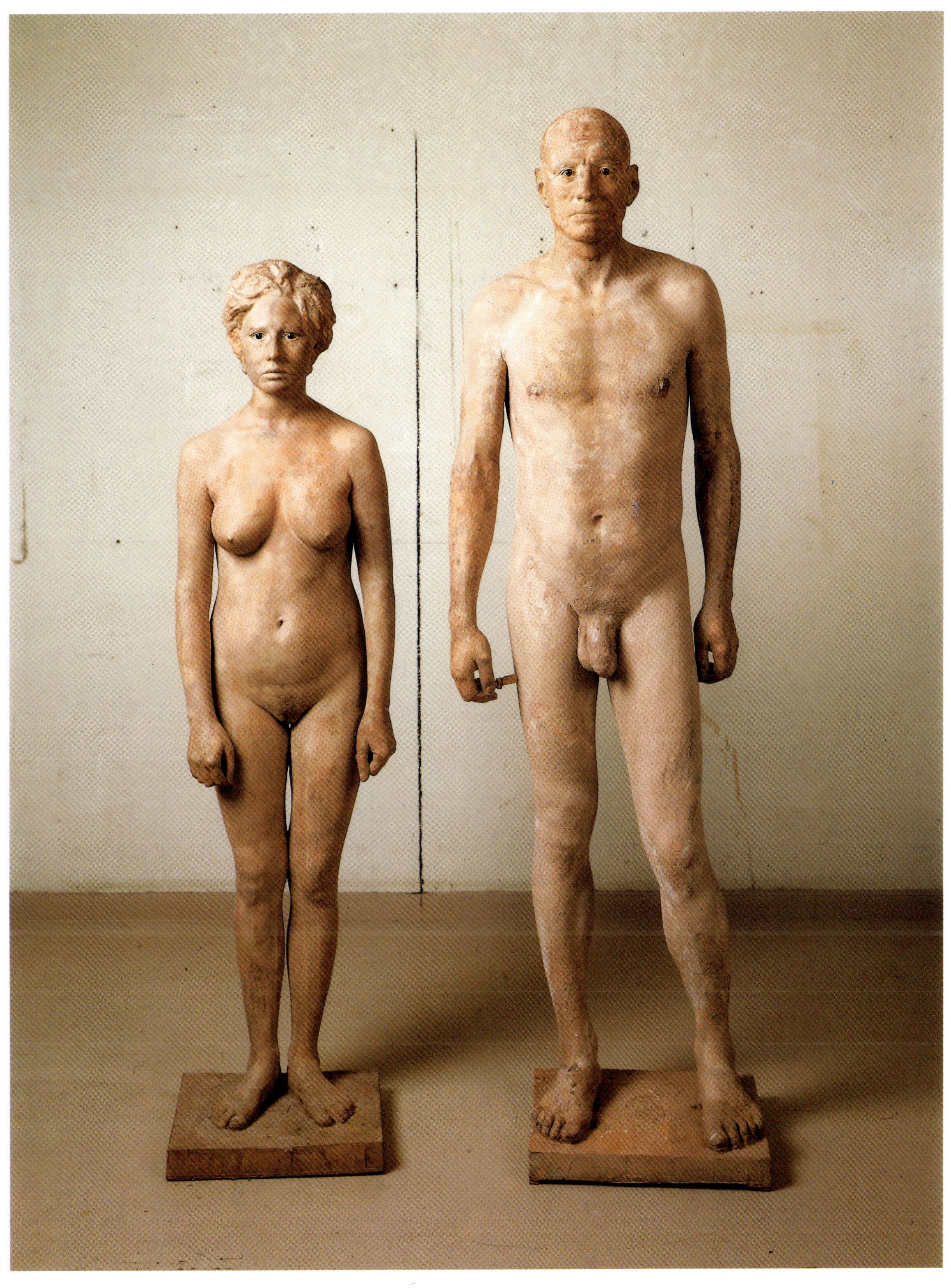

53. Man and Woman, *1968–1990. These two wooden sculptures that the artist considers unfinished are a landmark in his oeuvre. Over more than twenty years Antonio López made countless notes of various models in his impossible endeavour to arrive at a generic model of ordinary man. Instead of any idealisation or fidelity to previous canons of anatomical beauty, we are faced with the ambition to obtain a valid representation of the men and women of his times, the aspiration to gain access to that non-apprehensible dimension of cityscapes and domestic interiors. Few modern artists have faced such a profound challenge. Both images occupied a privileged position in the commemorative centenary exhibition of the Venice Biennial held in 1995.*

List of Plates

1. Sinforoso and Josefa, *1955.*
Oil on canvas, 62 × 88 cm.
Private collection.

2. Antonio and Carmen, *1956.*
Oil on canvas, 60.5 × 83.5 cm.
Private collection.

3. The Bride and Groom, *1955.*
Oil on canvas, 120 × 104 cm.
*Museo Nacional Centro de Arte Reina
Sofía, Madrid.*

4. Emilio and Angelines, *1961–1965.*
Oil on board, 107.5 × 98.5 cm.
Private collection.

5. Mari, *1961.*
Oil on board, 45 × 37 cm.
Private collection.

6. María, *1972.*
Pencil on paper, 70 × 53 cm.
Private collection, Madrid.

7. Carmencita Playing, *1960.*
Oil on canvas, 106.5 × 149.5 cm.
Private collection.

8. Francisco Carretero and Antonio
López Torres Conversing, *1959.*
Oil on board, 70 × 96 cm.
Private collection.

9. Calle Santa Rita, *1961.*
Oil on board, 62 × 88.5 cm.
Private collection.

10. Josefa, *1961.*
Lithograph, 35 × 50 cm.

11. Carmencita Dressed for Holy
Communion, *1960.*
Oil on board, 100 × 81 cm.
*Mr. & Mrs. Charles B. Wakeman
Collection.*

12. Room in Tomelloso, *1971–1972.*
Pencil on paper, 81 × 69 cm.
Private collection.

13. The House of Antonio López Torres,
1972–1975.
Pencil on paper, 82 × 68 cm.
Private collection.

14. Dead Girl, *1957.*
Oil on canvas, 90 × 105 cm.
Private collection.

15. The Lamp, *1959.*
Oil on board, 100 × 130 cm.
Private collection.

16. Figures in a House, *1967.*
Oil on board, 85 × 124 cm.
Fundación Juan March.

17. Mari in the Embajadores
Neighbourhood, *1962.*
Oil on board, 85 × 75 cm.
Private collection.

18. The Dresser, *1963.*
Oil on board, 200 × 100 cm.
Private collection.

19. Atocha, *1964.*
Oil on board, 95 × 105 cm.
Private collection, New York.

20. North Madrid Seen from
"La Maliciosa", *1964.*
Oil on board, 130 × 200 cm.
*The Chase Manhattan Bank Collection,
N. A.*

21. The China Cabinet, *1965–1966.*
Oil on board, 244 × 127 cm.
Private collection.

22. Icebox, *1966.*
Oil on canvas, 117 × 142 cm.
Private collection.

23. Hand Basin and Mirror, *1967.*
Oil on board, 98 × 83.5 cm.
Private collection, New York.

24. Lavatory Pan and Window,
1968–1971.
*Oil on paper, mounted on board,
143 × 93.5 cm.*
Masaveu Collection, Madrid.

25. Clothes in Soak, *1968.*
Oil on board, 80.5 × 74 cm.
Private collection.

26. Skinned Rabbit, *1972.*
Oil on board, 53 × 60.5 cm.
Private collection.

27. Leftovers, *1971.*
Pencil on paper, 42 × 54 cm.
*The Baltimore Museum of Art.
Donated by the Apple Hill Foundation
to The Thomas E. Benesch Memorial
Collection.*

28. Madrid Seen from Tío Pío Hill,
1962–1963.
Oil on board, 101.5 × 129.5 cm.
*Museo Nacional Centro de Arte Reina
Sofía, Madrid.*

29. Madrid Looking towards the
Observatory, *1965–1970.*
Oil on board, 122 × 244 cm.
Private collection.

30. South Madrid, *1965–1985.*
Oil on board, 153 × 244 cm.
Masaveu Collection, Madrid.

31. Madrid Seen from Torres Blancas,
1976–1982.
Oil on board, 145 × 244 cm.
Private collection.

32. Gran Vía, Clavel, *1977–1990.*
*Oil on canvas, mounted on board,
119.5 × 124 cm.*
Private collection.

33. Gran Vía, *1974–1981.*
Oil on board, 90.5 × 93.5 cm.
Private collection.

34. Campo del Moro, *1990.*
*Oil on canvas, mounted on board,
190 × 245 cm.*
Collection of the artist.

35. Supper, *1971–1980.*
Oil on board, 89 × 101 cm. Unfinished.
Collection of the artist.

36. Woman in the Bath, *1968.*
Oil on board, 107 × 166 cm.
Private collection.

37. Lucio's Roof Terrace, *1962–1990.*
Oil on board, 130.5 × 201.5 cm.
Work in progress.
Collection of the artist.

38. Afternoon Window, *1974–1982.*
Oil on board, 141 × 124 cm.
Joanne C. Kauzler Collection.

39. Studio with Three Doors,
1969–1970.
Pencil on paper, 98 × 113 cm.
Private collection.

40. Vase with Flowers and Wall, *1965.*
Oil on board, 44 × 37 cm.
Collection of the artist.

41. Electric Light, *1970.*
Pencil on paper, 122 × 100.5 cm.
Hamburger Kunsthalle,
Kupferstichkabinett, Hamburg.

42. The Vine, *1955.*
Oil on canvas, 48.5 × 48.5 cm.
Private collection.

43. Irises and Roses, *1977–1980.*
Oil on board, 66.5 × 66.5 cm.
Private collection.

44. Rear Garden, *1969.*
Oil on board, 86.5 × 100 cm.
Muromachi Fine Art Co., Ltd.
Collection.

45. Plum Tree, *1989.*
Pencil on paper, 73 × 87 cm.
Private collection.

46. Quince Tree, *1990.*
Pencil on paper, 104 × 120 cm.
Private collection, Madrid.

47. The Apparition of the Younger
Brother, *1959.*
Bronze. Edition 2/9, 57 × 79.5 cm.
Lerner & Lerner Collection.

48. The Apparition, *1963.*
Polychromed wood, 54.5 × 80 × 13.5 cm.
The Museum of Modern Art, New York.
Donated by Staempfli Gallery, 1965.

49. Sleeping Woman, *1963.*
Polychromed wood, 121 × 205 × 12 cm.
Private collection.

50. Mari, *1961.*
Bronze. Edition 1/4, 36.5 × 22.5 × 38 cm.
Private collection, Madrid.

51. María Standing, *1963.*
Polychromed wood, 75 × 27.5 × 30 cm.
Mr. & Mrs. Philip Clark Collection,
New York.

52. Carmencita, *1965–1968.*
Clay, 75 cm. approximate height.
Work in progress.

53. Man and Woman, *1968–1990.*
Wood. Man: 195 × 59 × 46 cm.;
Woman: 169 × 42.5 × 38 cm.
Unfinished.
Collection of the artist.

Recommended Reading

Antonio López García. Catalogue of the
anthological exhibition of painting,
sculpture and drawing. Museo Nacional
Centro de Arte Reina Sofía, Madrid, 1993.

Michael Brenson, Francisco Calvo Serraller and
Edward J. Sullivan, *Antonio López García,*
Lerner & Lerner, Madrid, 1990.

Miguel Fenández Braso, *La realidad en
Antonio López García,* Rayuela,
Madrid, 1978.